DANNII MARTIN is the author of healthy eating and lifestyle blog Hungry Healthy Happy, which provides healthier alternatives to everyone's favourite meals that don't sacrifice on taste. Dannii's down-to-earth approach and simple recipes provide inspiration to a growing audience of over 200,000 followers and she is consistently ranked as one of the UK's most influential bloggers.

As a mother to a toddler, Dannii knows how easy it can be to turn to convenience food, which is why she relies on her slow cooker to provide easy and healthy meals for her family that involve very little preparation.

After a health scare a few years ago, Dannii turned her life around with a total change of diet and exercise routine and her slow cooker featured heavily within that. Using the slow cooker to make family meals meant she had more time to dedicate to getting fit.

The Healthy Slow Cooker

Delicious, nutritious
eating made easy

Dannii Martin

ROBINSON

ROBINSON

First published in Great Britain in 2018 by Robinson

10 9 8 7 6 5 4 3 2 1

A CIP catalogue record for this book is available from the British Library.

ISBN: 978-1-47214-046-3

Designed and Typeset in Adelle by Andrew Barron at Thextension

Printed and bound in China by C&C

Papers used by Robinson are from well-managed forests and
other responsible sources.

Robinson
An imprint of Little, Brown Book Group
Carmelite House, 50 Victoria Embankment,
London EC4Y 0DZ

An Hachette UK Company

www.hachette.co.uk

www.littlebrown.co.uk

The recommendations given in this book are solely intended as
education and should not be taken as medical advice.

CONTENTS

The Benefits of Using a Slow Cooker

My journey to healthy eating and how my Slow Cooker played a part

Ten reasons to love your Slow Cooker

Top tips for choosing your Slow Cooker

Getting the most out of Slow Cooking

Two of the biggest challenges that people face when it comes to healthy eating are time and money, and the slow cooker can help with both of those. Your slow cooker can save you money by using cheaper cuts of meat, because it is cooked low and slow. They are also a great way to help reduce waste because you can use up whatever is left in your fridge. You will find that many of the recipes in this book can be easily adapted to use whatever vegetables you have that need using – so not only is using a slow cooker better for your bank balance, but reducing food waste is better for the environment, too. A slow cooker does not just save you money; it can also save you so much time in the kitchen. What could be easier than throwing it all in the slow cooker in the morning and walking in from work to the smell of your dinner cooked and ready to eat, or putting your slow cooker on before you go to bed and waking up to breakfast already cooked.

Healthy is a subjective word and what one person thinks is healthy, another person would not. But to me, being healthy means making small day-to-day changes. It is not about being restrictive and feeling deprived; it is about finding ways to increase your fruit and vegetable intake, making sure you are eating the right portion size and making lighter swaps where you can. The emphasis is on quality ingredients, but that are easily sourced from your local supermarket. I have tried to bring all of that to the 100 recipes in this book to show that healthy does not have to be boring.

When most of us think of a slow cooker meal, we think of a hearty meat stew that our grandparents would make. But, this book is here to show you that there is so much more that you can make in your slow cooker, and those meals can be light and fresh, as well as healthier versions of your favourite comfort foods. You can use your slow cooker to make everything from Mexican family favourites like Chicken Fajitas (page 91) and Nachos (page 131), to warming soups like Leek and Potato (page 39), from Saturday night burgers (pages 78 and 92), to Superfood Porridge (page 22), creamy mashed potatoes (pages 196 and 199), and so much more.

Slow cookers have made a huge comeback! No longer just thought of as an 1980s kitchen gadget for older people, they are loved by people of all ages who are looking to spend less time in the kitchen but not sacrifice on taste. Slow cookers practically cook the meal for you whilst you are free to get on with that never-ending list of things to do. Whether you love your slow cooker because it saves you time, is economical or is so easy to use, it is a must-have in any kitchen.

My journey to healthy eating and how my Slow Cooker played a part

Over ten years ago, I was finishing university and was terribly unhealthy. There is the typical student diet of takeaway and too much alcohol and then there is a level up from that, and that was where I was. The average day would consist of sugary cereal early in the morning (when I could be bothered to go to a class), a sugar-laden coffee when I got off the bus, a bacon sandwich for a second breakfast and then some crisps and chocolate between my morning classes – and that was all before lunch. Lunch was fast food or something stodgy from the university cafeteria and some cake for dessert, with a piece of fruit because that was my idea of healthy eating. Snacking through my afternoon classes with whatever I could get my hands on, because the afternoon energy slump had hit and I could barely stay awake, then it was time to go home and raid the kitchen. A ready meal or something beige and breaded from the freezer was on the menu as we started getting ready with pre-drinks for a night out. The evening only got more calorific from there with pints of cider and shots, but at least there was a lot of dancing to burn off some of the calories. And what is a night out without a takeaway on the way home? I wouldn't know, as we always got one. Pizza or fried chicken with cheesy chips covered in mayo and then that was me finally done and ready to go home and sleep it off. Ready to wake up and start it all over again. Some days I was having over 4000 calories a day, with the only exercise being walking towards more food. It's no wonder I felt awful all the time, had no energy and the weight was piling on.

Then one day a health scare gave me the kick I needed to make a change. I couldn't carry on eating the way I was and abusing my body like that, so I made a vow to make small healthy changes every day to improve my health, and one of those changes was to cook everything from scratch.

Being a poor student with not much time and being a total novice in the kitchen, I decided to get a slow cooker. I figured it could do all the work for me and I could sneak in some extra vegetables to my diet, which was one of my goals. I would put the slow cooker on in the morning before classes and come home to dinner already cooked for me – no need to order a takeaway. The leftovers I took the next day for lunch, if it was something I could eat cold or add to a sandwich or salad, and although my recipe repertoire was small in the beginning, I soon started experimenting with more until I had plenty that I could add to my meal plan – many of which you will find in this book.

My philosophy when it came to healthy eating was that I didn't want to give up any of my favourite foods. I wanted to create healthier versions of them, which is why you will still find comforting pasta dishes, burgers, tacos, stews, desserts and takeaway favourites. I just found ways to make them a little lighter, and save myself some time by cooking them in the slow cooker – time that I could spend introducing some exercise into my routine.

Cooking my own meals from scratch with very little preparation time had a huge impact on my health and not only was I seeing the number on the scale going down, but I felt amazing. I had discovered a new love and appreciation for food, rather than just using it as an emotional crutch. I was still enjoying variations of my favourite meals and I had plenty of time left over to work on all the other things that were going to contribute to a healthier and happier me. My slow cooker literally changed my life.

Once I reached my goal, 7 stone lost, and finished university, the slow cooker certainly didn't get packed away. It was still used several times a week as I entered the working world and had even less time to prepare meals. Fast forward several years and I was pregnant with our first child and the slow cooker became my best friend. When morning sickness hit me with a big thump in the first trimester, it was hard for me to be around food for too long. I turned to anything that took barely any time at all to prepare and I could keep it warm in the slow cooker until the sickness had passed and I was ready to eat. Being totally honest, the first twelve weeks of pregnancy I barely did any cooking because the sickness was debilitating at times, so my husband took over the roll as head chef. A self-confessed novice cook, he certainly lacks confidence in the kitchen and he prefers anything that can just be thrown together and is very hard to mess up – the slow cooker was perfect for him. Already having a back catalogue of slow cooker recipes to turn to, he has since said that he loved being able to cook a delicious meal for us that hardly took any effort.

Then, when our daughter was born, our slow cooker was practically a life saver. So much so that we bought a second one so that we could cook the main meal and the side in it. As for most first-time parents, the first few months were a whirlwind of sleepless nights, googling absolutely everything the baby did, being trapped under a snoozing/feeding baby and taking photographs of every hilarious facial expression. There was no time to be stuck in the kitchen when there was this tiny person in our lives, growing up way too fast. Rather than ordering takeaway night after night, we put the slow cooker to work. Pregnancy had not been kind to my body and I gave in to pretty much every pregnancy craving that I had, so not only did I have very little time to cook, I had some extra weight to shift too. I took things back to basics and cooked all of my favourite slow cooker meals that had helped me the first time round. We had batch-cooked loads in the final nesting weeks of pregnancy, so we had those to fall back on for lunches and we had a freshly cooked slow cooker meal every evening. I don't know what we would have done without the slow cooker. Actually, I do: we would have ordered a lot more pizza.

Many of these recipes are baby friendly too and we used them during baby-led weaning. There are lots of recipes in this book that are marked as 'kid-approved' and that means either my daughter has loved eating them (she was chief taste tester when creating this book) or they are recipes that older kids will enjoy.

What I hope you have taken from reading about my journey to health is that a slow cooker really is for everyone. Whether you are a student who wants to make healthier changes, or you are climbing the career ladder with very little time to cook, a kitchen novice, pregnant or a parent with a never ending to-do list, the slow cooker can help you make healthier versions of your favourite foods while spending much less time in the kitchen.

Ten reasons to love your Slow Cooker

1 IT SAVES YOU TIME Although the recipes in this book differ in terms of preparation and cooking time, I have tried to keep them as simple and as quick to prepare as possible, because that is what the slow cooker is all about. Some of the recipes require a little cooking (or browning) before the ingredients go into the slow cooker, but the majority of the recipes just involve mixing the ingredients together and turning it on, which is why a slow cooker will save you so much time in the kitchen.

2 IT KEEPS YOUR HOUSE COOL There is nothing worse than having your oven on for an hour during the heat of summer, so avoid that by using your slow cooker. Do not sweat over the stove – just throw everything in the slow cooker and enjoy the nice weather outside. Recipes like Chipotle Pulled Chicken Burgers (page 92), BBQ Turkey and Avocado Wraps (page 50) and 'Roasted' Vegetable Salad (page 174) are summer favourites.

3 YOU CAN'T RUIN YOUR DINNER The slow cooker is made for people with a busy life. If you are late home from work, or you were too busy helping your kids finish their homework to concentrate on dinner, the slow cooker does not mind as it is near impossible to ruin whatever you are cooking in there. Get yourself a timer and it will switch off exactly when you want it to as well.

4 THE SMELL THAT GREETS YOU You know when you walk into a restaurant and you are greeted with all those delicious smells that fill the room? Well, using your slow cooker is exactly the same, and coming home from work you will smell your dinner as soon as you open the door, or maybe before you even reach your house. Equally, if you make one of the breakfast recipes, the smell of Carrot Cake Porridge (page 26) or Apple, Cinnamon and Vanilla Oats (page 25) will be enough to get you out of bed in the morning.

5 IT CAN SAVE YOU MONEY Now I have got your attention! Not only can a slow cooker save you money by using up what is in your fridge or making the most of cheaper cuts of meat, but it also uses less electricity than the oven.

6 IT CAN HELP WHEN FEEDING A CROWD If you have quite a few people to serve food to, like at a party or at Christmas time, then you will quickly realise how little space you have in your oven and on your hob. Your slow cooker has got you covered, as you can make one of the dishes in there. The Red Onion and Tomato Chutney (page 192) is a real crowd pleaser at parties, and you can also use the slow cooker to make various side dishes (see pages 179–208) whilst you cook the main meal in the oven.

7 IT HELPS YOU TO AVOID ORDERING TAKEAWAY With demanding jobs, before- and after-school activities, and even the family dog having a social life, the time we have left to spend in the kitchen is less than ever before. The temptation to just order a pizza when you walk in the door is strong, when even the thought of having to cook something is exhausting. If you have spent five minutes in the morning putting something in the slow cooker before heading out the door, dinner is waiting and you do not need to order a pizza, saving you calories and money – it's a win-win!

8 IT MAKES THE TASTIEST MEAT DISHES In my opinion, slow cooking is the best way to cook meat. It just falls apart when you put your fork into it, and cooking it over time really allows for the meat to take on all the flavour from the seasonings. Perfect examples of this are the Lamb Rogan Josh (page 107) and Seasame Beef and Broccoli (page 103).

9 IT IS A GREAT WAY TO HIDE VEGETABLES If you are cooking for fussy eaters, then a slow cooker can help you to hide some extra vegetables in their meals. Slow cooking makes vegetables really soft and harder to notice. Try making Butternut Squash Macaroni Cheese (page 141) or Hidden Vegetable Pasta Sauce (page 138) and see if anyone notices that the dishes are packed full of vegetables.

10 LESS CLEANING UP As someone who hates washing up (doesn't everyone?), this is my favourite benefit of using a slow cooker – there is minimal washing up. If you make one of the recipes that does not need any pre-cooking, then all you have to wash up is a chopping board and knife and your slow cooker bowl. Less time washing up means more time to enjoy what you love in life.

Top tips for choosing your Slow Cooker

If you do not have a slow cooker yet and you are looking to buy your first one, or if you are just looking for an upgrade, then there are some different features to consider. Slow cookers come in a wide range of sizes, with different functions, and they vary greatly in price. Finding the right one for you depends on what you are going to be using it for.

1 GET ONE WITH A TRANSPARENT LID As tempting as it can be to lift the lid on the slow cooker to have a peek or a sniff, doing so can lose a lot of precious heat and make the cooking time longer. Get a slow cooker with a transparent lid so you can check how things are going without letting the heat escape.

2 DO NOT BUY ANYTHING TOO LARGE Small- or medium-sized slow cookers are your best bet, as once you move on to the larger models there can be problems with heat distribution and cooking times can then vary. I would recommend getting two medium-sized slow cookers rather than one larger one if you are cooking for a big family. All the recipes in this book have been made in a 3-litre slow cooker and this is usually enough to feed four people, or two with leftovers. Remember, you cannot fill a slow cooker all the way to the top; however, for the best results you need to have your slow cooker half full, so buy one that suits your needs.

3 CHOOSE THE RIGHT SHAPE FOR YOU Slow cookers usually come in round or oval shapes, and whilst neither is better than the other, which one you choose depends on what you will mostly be using the cooker for. Whole chickens will fit better in an oval slow cooker; however, stews and curries, for example, will cook perfectly in both. It is best to buy a shape that will fit in your cupboards or slot in between your other gadgets on your kitchen counter.

4 CONSIDER GETTING ONE WITH A TIMER Although you can get plug-in timers pretty cheaply, consider getting a slow cooker with a timer already built in. Having a timer means that you can have your meal ready for exactly when you want it. Unless you can guarantee you will be home to switch it off, having a timer means your food does not become mushy and over-cooked, although slow cooker meals are much more forgiving than oven-cooked.

5 CHOOSE ONE WITH A VARIETY OF COOKING SETTINGS
Some of the cheaper slow cookers only have a HIGH cooking setting; however, for slow cooking a LOW setting is a must in my opinion. Cooking on a lower heat over a longer period of time allows meat to get really tender. Having a LOW setting also allows you to put the cooker on before you go out for the day without having to have a timer. Some also have a WARMING setting too. This is perfect for keeping your food warm until you are ready to eat it, without it carrying on cooking.

6 DECIDE IF YOU WILL BENEFIT FROM A BROWNING FEATURE
If you have a little more money to spend on a slow cooker, consider getting one that has a hob-safe insert. Instead of browning meat in a separate pan, you can put the slow cooker bowl directly on the hob to brown the meat and then put it back into the slow cooker housing to do the rest of the cooking. This saves on washing up, but that does come at a price as they are considerably more expensive.

7 CONSIDER WHICH SAFETY FEATURES YOU REQUIRE Cool wall models are safer to touch whilst in use and are the better option if you have children in your kitchen. They are also generally more energy efficient, as they don't let the heat escape out the sides.

Getting the most out of Slow Cooking

Now you have chosen your perfect slow cooker, it is time to get the most out of it. Here are a few simple tips to help you use your slow cooker to its full potential.

1 Do not remove the lid too often, or at all if possible, or you will lose heat and extend the cooking time. Around 20–30 minutes is added every time you lift the lid.

2 Liquid does not escape from a slow cooker, so if you are looking to adapt a recipe to make in your slow cooker, you will probably need to reduce the amount of liquid used. You need just enough liquid to cover the meat/vegetables.

3 If you have too much liquid and you want to thicken up the sauce, you can use cornflour or arrowroot. Just remove a spoonful of the liquid and put it in a bowl with 1–2 tbsp of arrowroot or cornflour. Whisk well to remove any lumps, then add it back to the slow cooker and stir.

4 A little créme fraîche or yoghurt stirred into stews, curries or soups at the end will make them creamy without adding a lot of extra calories.

5 Slow cookers can vary greatly, so the time it takes to cook a dish can vary, too. Always consult the manual of your slow cooker to get a guide on cooking times and temperature.

6 Your slow cooker should be at room temperature when it gets turned on. So, if you have prepared everything the night before, store it in a different container and put in the fridge overnight, then tip the ingredients into the slow cooker bowl in the morning before cooking.

7 Pasta and rice generally do not do well being cooked over a long time, as they turn to mush, so they need to be added towards the end in most cases. The same goes for fresh herbs.

8 Although I have included plenty of recipes that are cooked on high for a shorter amount of time (not everyone wants to wait all day for their food to be ready), cooking on low gives the best and most delicious results. The slow gentle heat really brings out the flavours.

9 Be aware that low and high temperatures vary depending on what slow cooker you are using, so please use timings as a guide only and always check that the food is cooked through before eating.

10 Smaller chunks are better, especially when it comes to root vegetables, which can sometimes take longer than meat to cook in a slow cooker. Cut them into smaller chunks for best results. You should also try and put them at the bottom, as ingredients at the bottom of the slow cooker cook faster.

11 Browning the meat can give it a better colour: slow cooking can sometimes drain the colour from meat and make it look a bit dull, so if you are looking to impress dinner guests with the way the dish looks too, you might want to brown the meat first to give it some colour.

12 Use dried herbs as much as possible. Fresh herbs are great for garnish, or for stirring through right at the end, but when cooked over a long period of time they can become brown and limp. Dried herbs are a much better option because their flavour is released over time. Dried herbs are much more budget friendly too, as they will not get forgotten about at the back of the fridge.

13 If you have any leftovers, make sure you transfer them to a separate container to allow them to cool before putting them in the fridge or freezer. This is because the slow cooker retains its heat for a long period of time, so if you allow food to slowly cool down inside it, bacteria can build up.

14 Never add cold water straight to a slow cooker bowl whilst it is still hot as it may crack.

15 Make sure you preheat your slow cooker before adding food to it. All the times stated in the recipes are calculated from food going into a preheated cooker. Adding cooked food to a cold slow cooker will also cool it down and take an extra 10–15 minutes for it to warm up again.

Healthy Eating with Your Slow Cooker

The benefits of eating more meat-free meals

Healthy eating on a budget with a Slow Cooker

Your slow cooker can be your best friend in the kitchen when it comes to healthy eating. There are many ways that it can help you and here are just a few.

1 Many slow cooker recipes require little to no fat to be used in the cooking, as everything just bubbles away in the slow cooker.

2 Not only can you cook some incredible meat-free recipes in a slow cooker, but if you are cooking a meat dish, a slow cooker allows you to use less meat because it really brings out the flavour of a small amount. You can bulk it out with extra vegetables too. Just remember, when you cook meat on the hob, a lot of the fat drains away, but this doesn't happen in a slow cooker, so it's best to trim off as much of the fat as you can to make it a lighter dish.

3 Slow cookers are great for people who don't love cooking. It's hard to eat healthily if you don't enjoy cooking as it's more tempting to buy convenience food and avoid cooking altogether. But a slow cooker takes all the hassle out of cooking, and they are perfect for people that aren't confident in the kitchen, too.

4 Because most slow cooker dishes are cooked in their own juices (rather than adding fat) and at a lower temperature, it locks in a lot of the vitamins and minerals that would otherwise be lost when using other cooking methods.

5 It is so easy to bulk out slow cooker meals with vegetables without really noticing. This means it's a great way to increase your family's vegetable intake without changing what they eat too much. Try the Hidden Vegetable Pasta Sauce (page 138) for a meal with a secret health boost.

6 A slow cooker can help you to get a meal on the table for your family with minimal effort, which means you are much less likely to order a pizza or put a ready-meal in the oven. Even better, make a couple of big batch recipes at the weekend like the Low-carb Veggie-packed Lasagna (page 127) or Creamy Coconut Lentils (page 146) and freeze them in individual portions for easy meals that will help you to avoid convenience junk food.

7 Lean cuts of meat taste better when cooked in the slow cooker. Lean cuts aren't very tender and can be a little dry when cooked other ways, but cooking them in the slow cooker keeps them moist and tender, and helps you cut down on fat.

8 Rather than standing over the hob, stirring and waiting for dinner to cook, you can let the slow cooker do all the work and use the time you have saved to fit in a quick workout.

9 Takeaways can be a huge downfall for many, but it's so easy to make healthier versions of takeaway favourites like Sweet and Sour Chicken (page 69), Lamb Rogan Josh (page 107) and Leafy Green Madras (page 145).

The benefits of eating more meat-free meals

I am not here to tell you to give up meat and make all of your meals meat-free; however, the benefits of going meat-free for a few meals a week, or even a whole day, are huge. Meat- and dairy-free meals don't have to be boring and there are plenty of ways you can add flavour with herbs and spices and add texture with chunky vegetables. Well over half of the recipes in this book are meatless – many of them vegan too.

1 HEART HEALTH Many fatty red meats and processed meats are high in saturated fat, which raises bad HDL cholesterol and contributes towards heart disease. Swap meaty foods for vegetarian versions, like the Mushroom Bolognese (page 162) or the Lentil Ragu (page 165) for a meat-free alternative.

2 HELP THE ENVIRONMENT It's time that we started thinking about future generations and the impact that the way we eat is going to have on them. It's a scary fact that raising cattle for beef and milk releases more greenhouse gases into the air than all the cars on the road. Eating more vegetarian and vegan meals means that there is less demand for meat products, which could therefore have a huge positive impact on the environment over time.

3 WEIGHT LOSS If your goal is to drop a few pounds, or just feel more comfortable in your clothes, then swapping out the meat for a vegetarian alternative can go a long way to helping with that. Swap meat for beans, as in the Chipotle Black Bean Stew (page 153), for a meal that is just as filling but lower in fat.

4 TRYING SOMETHING NEW You will be amazed at how many new favourite meals you'll discover by making some meat-free changes. It is now easier than ever to eat more vegetarian meals, with supermarkets stocking a much wider range of specialist products, introducing world food aisles, and sourcing fruit and vegetables a little different from the norm. Just be careful to watch out for processed food – just because it is meat-free it does not mean that it isn't loaded with junk.

5 ENERGY BOOST Wholegrains and legumes keep you fuller for longer and offer you plenty of energy without the blood sugar crash that simple carbs will give.

6 SAVES MONEY Plant-based alternatives like mushrooms, beans and lentils are cheaper than meat and can therefore save you money on your food shop.

7 MORE COLOURFUL MEALS They say that the first bite is with the eye and let's face it, meat looks pretty bland. Adding more vegetables to your diet, and more vegetarian meals, can make your meals look much more colourful and therefore more appetising.

Healthy eating on a budget with a Slow Cooker

One of the main things that stops people from making healthier changes to their diet is money. Whilst healthy eating can be expensive, it doesn't have to be and these tips will help you make your food budget go a little bit further and also help you to use your slow cooker for budget-friendly meals.

1 BUY CHEAPER CUTS OF MEAT You don't have to splurge on tender cuts of meat when using a slow cooker, because cooking meat at a low temperature for a longer period of time makes cheaper cuts of meat much easier to chew.

2 BULK MEALS OUT WITH BEANS, LENTILS AND VEGETABLES
These are much cheaper than meat, so by bulking your meals out
with them you can save a lot of money. If you still want a meaty
flavour in dishes such as lentil and bean stews, then adding a
little diced bacon can go a long way.

3 COOK MEALS IN BULK You can batch cook many of the meals
in this book using a slow cooker and make use of supermarket
special offers. Chicken on offer? Cook up a batch of the Chipotle
Pulled Chicken (page 92) and freeze it to add to sandwiches and
salads. Canned beans available in bulk? Make the Chipotle Black
Bean Stew (page 153) as it freezes really well and has so many uses.

4 REDUCE YOUR ENERGY BILLS Slow cookers use less energy
than the stove, which means that you can save money to spend
on more ingredients for delicious healthy meals.

5 PLAN YOUR MEALS Meal planning is a great way to save
money on food, because you are not tempted to buy convenience
food if nothing else is planned. As slow cooker meals have to be
prepped ahead of time, the planning is already done.

6 COOK IN JUST ONE POT Most of the recipes in this book just
require the one pot in the slow cooker, which means less washing
up. Less washing up saves using the dishwasher, and means less
water and washing-up liquid are needed, which is also better for
the environment.

7 BUY LARGER CUTS OF MEAT Buying larger cuts of meat from
the butcher can work out much more economical. Buy a whole
chicken to cook and shred up for meals (on page 57), rather than
chicken breasts.

8 RAID YOUR FRIDGE AND CUPBOARD Instead of going to the
supermarket to buy new ingredients, see what you can make
with what you already have. The Minestrone Soup (page 44) and
Fridge-Raid Ratatouille (page 173) are perfect for this.

9 COOK FROM SCRATCH Slow cooker recipes require little to no pre-prepared or cooked food, which means you have to make everything from scratch and that works out cheaper.

10 SAVE VEGETABLE CUTTINGS When peeling vegetables like carrots and parsnips, save the trimmings and put them in a freezer bag to make stock. Store in the freezer, adding to the bag until it is full. When it is full, put them in the slow cooker with some water and seasoning and cook on low for around 8 hours. Strain, then store in air-tight jars in the fridge. Less food waste and no need to buy expensive stock cubes.

11 EAT SEASONALLY Eating out of season can really push up the cost of your food shop. So whilst it's tempting to want to make Strawberry Chia Jam (page 30) throughout the year, keep it to when strawberries are in season to keep your food budget down, and enjoy fruit and veg at their best.

12 GET YOUR OATS Oats are nutritious, filling and budget friendly, not to mention versatile. Try to eat them for breakfast a few times a week – the Apple, Cinnamon and Vanilla Oats (page 25) and the Carrot Cake Porridge (page 26) are a great place to start.

13 KNOW YOUR HERBS AND SPICES If you shop in the world food aisles or in international supermarkets, you can fill up your herb and spice rack for less. Herbs and spices are a great way to add lots of flavour to your meals without stretching your food budget.

14 CONTROL YOUR PORTIONS Many of us are eating almost double the portion size we should be. Eating more sensible portions and freezing any leftovers means your food budget will go further.

If you were not on board with slow cooking before, then I hope you are now. Now it is time to dive right into 100 delicious and healthy slow cooker recipes.

Conversion charts

WEIGHT

METRIC	IMPERIAL
25g	1oz
50g	2oz
75g	3oz
100g	4oz
150g	5oz
175g	6oz
200g	7oz
225g	8oz
250g	9oz
300g	10oz
350g	12oz
400g	14oz
450g	1lb

MEASUREMENTS

METRIC	IMPERIAL
5cm	2in
10cm	4in
13cm	5in
15cm	6in
18cm	7in
20cm	8in
25cm	10in
30cm	12in

LIQUIDS

METRIC	IMPERIAL	US CUP
5ml	1 tsp	1 tsp
15ml	1 tbsp	1 tbsp
50ml	2fl oz	3 tbsp
60ml	2½fl oz	¼ cup
75ml	3fl oz	⅓ cup
100ml	4fl oz	scant ½ cup
125ml	4½ oz	½ cup
150ml	5fl oz	⅔ cup
200ml	7fl oz	scant 1 cup
250ml	9fl oz	1 cup
300ml	½ pint	1¼ cups
350ml	12fl oz	1⅓ cups
400ml	¾ pint	1¾ cups
500ml	17fl oz	2 cups
600ml	1 pt	2½ cups

Breakfast

What better way to start your day than with a big bowl of superfood-topped porridge?

SUPERFOOD PORRIDGE

SERVES 2
Vegetarian

PREP TIME
5 minutes

COOK TIME
6 hours on low

INGREDIENTS
90g rolled oats
750ml almond milk
2 tbsp chia seeds
2 tbsp honey
1 tsp vanilla extract
4 tbsp pomegranate seeds
35g blueberries
2 tbsp flaked almonds

The term 'superfood' is often applied to anything remotely healthy, but the blueberries and pomegranate add lots of nutrients and texture to this creamy porridge. The chia seeds add protein and give it an almost jelly-like texture, and you get plenty of crunch and healthy fats from the almonds. I think even Goldilocks would love this porridge, and we all know how fussy she was.

1 Preheat your slow cooker to low.
2 Put the oats, almond milk, chia seeds, honey and vanilla extract in the slow cooker and cook for 6 hours.
3 Serve in bowls and top with pomegranate seeds, blueberries and almonds.

NUTRITIONAL FACT
Packed with antioxidants, blueberries are also high in vitamin C and potassium.

TOP TIP
The best way to remove seeds from a pomegranate is to roll the fruit to loosen the seeds. Score around the middle and tear open the halves. Hold the pomegranate face down over a bowl and strike the back with a spoon, squeezing slightly.

Apple and cinnamon just scream autumn, and although you would often find them together in an apple pie, here they are paired in a creamy bowl of oats for a comforting way to start the day.

APPLE, CINNAMON AND VANILLA OATS

SERVES 2
Vegetarian

PREP TIME
5 minutes

COOK TIME
6 hours on low

INGREDIENTS
2 small apples, diced,
  plus extra to serve
90g rolled oats
250ml skimmed milk
2 tbsp maple syrup
1 tsp vanilla extract
½ tsp ground cinnamon
walnuts, broken into pieces,
  to serve

Porridge is a breakfast staple in the winter, but plain oats can quickly get boring. Throw these ingredients in the slow cooker before you go to bed and wake up to what is basically a big hug in a bowl. Sweet chunks of apple, spicy cinnamon and warming vanilla, all stirred into creamy oats.

1 Preheat your slow cooker to low.
2 Put the apples, oats, milk, maple syrup, vanilla extract and cinnamon in the slow cooker along with 250ml water. Stir together, and cook for 6 hours.
3 Serve in bowls and top with walnuts and extra apple.

NUTRITIONAL FACT
Cinnamon is a powerful antioxidant that can help to regulate blood sugar.

If you ever wake up craving dessert for breakfast (and I mean, who doesn't?), then this bowl of oats is for you.

CARROT CAKE PORRIDGE

SERVES 4
Vegetarian

PREP TIME
5 minutes

COOK TIME
3 hours on high

INGREDIENTS
85g rolled oats
750ml skimmed milk
2 tbsp maple syrup
1 tbsp vanilla extract
1 large carrot, finely grated
½ tsp ground cinnamon
½ tsp ground nutmeg
½ tsp ground ginger
crushed pecans, to serve (optional)

Having cake for breakfast is usually a bit of a no-no (we have all been there); however, this has all the flavour you know and love from carrot cake but in a healthy and balanced breakfast.

1 Preheat your slow cooker to high.
2 Put the oats, milk, maple syrup, vanilla extract, grated carrot, cinnamon, nutmeg and ginger in the slow cooker and cook for 3 hours.
3 Serve in bowls and top with crushed pecans, if you wish.

NUTRITIONAL FACT
Carrots are one of the best sources of beta-carotene, which the body converts to vitamin A.

Granola is a tasty and quick breakfast option when you want something sweet in the morning.
This recipe makes a big batch of 10 portions and stores well in an airtight jar for a couple of weeks – if you can resist it for that long.

DARK CHOCOLATE AND CHERRY GRANOLA

SERVES 10
Vegetarian and *Kid-approved*

PREP TIME
5 minutes

COOK TIME
2 hours on high

INGREDIENTS
cooking oil spray
360g rolled oats
70g pecans
100g sunflower seeds
1 tsp ground ginger
a pinch of salt
75g coconut oil
125ml maple syrup
1 tbsp vanilla extract
60g dried cherries
100g dark chocolate (at least 70% cocoa content), chopped into chunks
milk or yoghurt, to serve

You cannot go wrong with chocolate and cherry together – it is such a classic and delicious combination and kids will love having chocolate for breakfast in this weekend treat. It is sweet, but still protein packed from the pecans, making it a good breakfast option, even if it does feel a bit indulgent.

1 Spray the inside of the slow cooker with cooking oil spray and preheat it to high.
2 Add the oats, pecans, sunflower seeds, ginger and salt to the slow cooker.
3 Melt the coconut oil in a saucepan over low heat, then add the maple syrup and vanilla. Pour over the oats in the slow cooker and stir. Cook for 2 hours, with the lid slightly off to let steam out. Stir every 30 minutes. Spread on a tray for an hour to crisp up.
4 Once the granola has cooled, stir through the dried cherries and chocolate chunks. Serve bowls of granola with milk or yoghurt.

NUTRITIONAL FACT
Studies show that the flavanols in cocoa can improve blood flow to the skin, protecting it from sun-induced damage.

If you have strawberries at the back of the fridge that are on their way out, chop them up and throw them in the slow cooker for an easy, healthier jam that will have your family fighting over it at the breakfast table.

STRAWBERRY CHIA JAM

SERVES 2
Vegetarian and *Kid-approved*

PREP TIME
5 minutes

COOK TIME
2 hours on high

INGREDIENTS
20 strawberries, hulled and diced
2 tbsp honey or maple syrup
1 tbsp lemon juice
2 tbsp chia seeds

There's no need to stand over the hob watching jam bubbling away, as the slow cooker does all the work for you. Not only does adding chia seeds thicken up the jam, but they add some protein too. Perfect spread on some crumpets on a lazy Sunday morning.

1 Preheat your slow cooker to high.
2 Put the strawberries, honey (or maple syrup) and lemon juice in the slow cooker and cook for 2 hours.
3 Mash the strawberries using a potato masher until you have a chunky purée, then stir in the chia seeds. Allow the jam to cool and thicken before serving.

NUTRITIONAL FACT
Chia seeds are rich in fibre, omega-3 fats, protein, vitamins and minerals.

Fill up your freezer with these breakfast burritos and you will always have a hearty and tasty breakfast on the go.

BREAKFAST BURRITOS

SERVES 10
Vegetarian and *Freezer-friendly*

PREP TIME
15 minutes

COOK TIME
6 hours on low, plus 5 minutes

INGREDIENTS

For the filling

1 tsp olive oil
2 potatoes, peeled and diced
1 large onion, peeled and diced
4 vegetarian sausages, diced
1 yellow pepper, finely diced
12 eggs
125ml skimmed milk
sea salt and black pepper

To serve

10 flour tortillas
5 large salad tomatoes, diced
1 avocado, diced
3 tbsp pickled jalapeños, diced
40g Cheddar cheese, grated
a handful of fresh coriander,
  chopped

These are not just a rushed breakfast option though, because they are great for feeding a crowd. Just put everything on the table and let everyone build their own burritos over a leisurely Mexican-inspired brunch.

1 Preheat your slow cooker to low.
2 Heat the olive oil in a frying pan, add the potatoes, onion, sausages and pepper, and gently cook for 5 minutes, until the onion is softened.
3 In a bowl, whisk together the eggs and milk and season with salt and pepper.
4 Spray the inside of the slow cooker with oil, then pour in the egg mixture. Add the potato mixture and gently stir. Cook for 6 hours, or until the egg is cooked.
5 Divide the egg mixture between the tortillas, sprinkle over the toppings and fold up. Either eat straight away or wrap in clingfilm and freeze.

FACT
Did you know, the word burrito means 'little donkey' in Spanish.

A great throw-it-all-in breakfast dish, this breakfast egg casserole is easy to adapt, a great way to use up leftovers and a good way to feed a crowd for breakfast.

BREAKFAST EGG CASSEROLE

SERVES 8
Vegetarian

PREP TIME
10 minutes

COOK TIME
6 hours on low

INGREDIENTS
cooking oil spray
12 eggs
250ml skimmed milk
½ tsp crushed chilli flakes
2 green peppers, diced
16 cherry tomatoes, quartered
1 onion, peeled and diced
40g Cheddar cheese, grated
sea salt and black pepper
sliced avocado, to serve (optional)

If your weekends are just as busy as the working week, then save yourself some time and make this for brunch.

1 Spray the slow cooker with a little oil and preheat it to low.
2 In a bowl, whisk together the eggs, milk and chilli flakes and season with salt and pepper. Pour into the slow cooker.
3 Add all the remaining ingredients (except the avocado) and gently stir.
4 Cook for 6 hours, or until set. Slice into 8 pieces and serve with avocado, if desired.

TOP TIP
Keep your eggs refrigerated. They age more at room temperature in one day than they do in the fridge over one week.

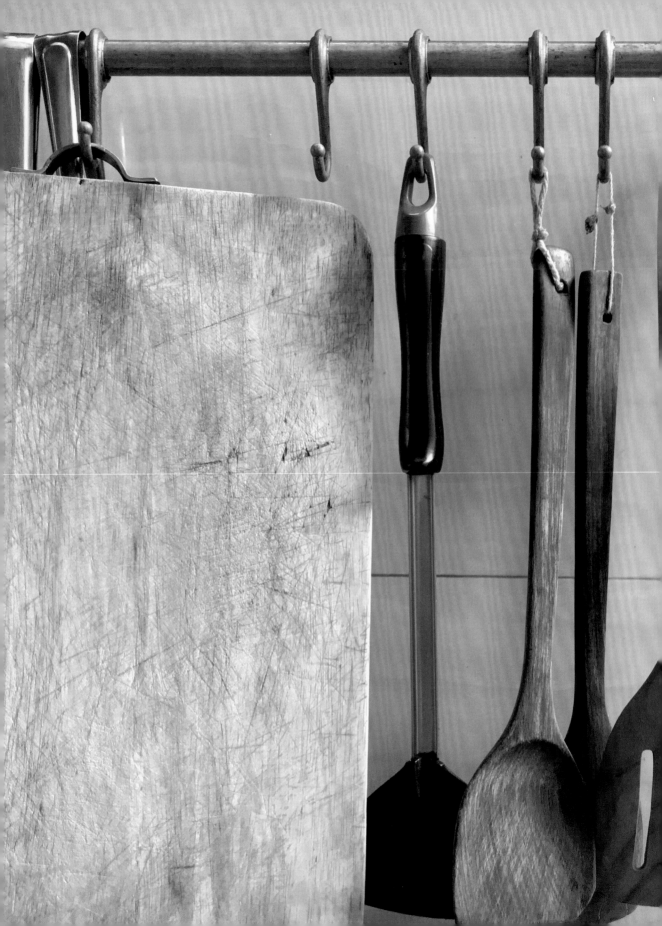

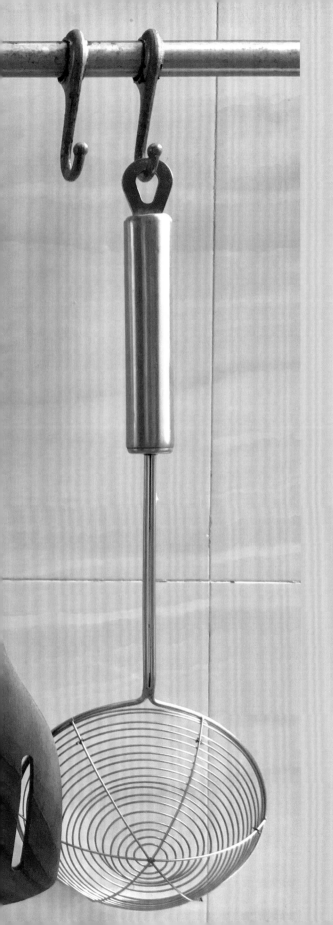

Soup

A smooth and creamy vegetable-packed soup that is best simply served with a chunk of crusty bread.

LEEK AND POTATO SOUP

SERVES 4
Vegetarian

PREP TIME
10 minutes

COOK TIME
4 hours on high

INGREDIENTS
3 leeks, chopped
3 medium potatoes, peeled and
   diced into small chunks
1 litre vegetable stock
2 garlic cloves, crushed
1 tbsp 0% fat crème fraîche
sea salt and black pepper
croutons, to serve

This is one soup that everyone should know how to make and is a serious budget saver at the end of the month.

1 Preheat your slow cooker to high.
2 Put all of the ingredients, except for the crème fraîche, in the slow cooker and cook for 4 hours.
3 Use a hand blender to blend until smooth, then stir through the crème fraiche. Season to taste and serve with croutons.

NUTRITIONAL FACT
Leeks are an excellent source of vitamins A, C, B6, E and K. They are also rich in copper, iron, magnesium, calcium and omega-3 fatty acids.

BONUS RECIPE
Chill any leftovers of this and serve cold (it is called vichyssoise) for a delicious summertime lunch.

Two flavours do not come more perfectly matched than tomato and basil and this simple slow cooker twist on a family recipe is one of the best ways to make use of fresh tomatoes.

TOMATO AND BASIL SOUP

SERVES 2
Vegan

PREP TIME
10 minutes

COOK TIME
2 hours on high

INGREDIENTS
6 plum tomatoes, diced
3 garlic cloves, crushed
1 onion, diced
1 potato, peeled and diced
1 carrot, peeled and diced
8 basil leaves, finely chopped,
   plus whole leaves to serve
500ml vegetable stock
sea salt and black pepper

To experience this soup in all it is glory, make sure you use really ripe seasonal tomatoes.

1 Preheat your slow cooker to high.
2 Put all the ingredients in a slow cooker and cook for 2 hours.
3 Use a hand blender to blend until smooth, season to taste and serve.

FACT
There are over 10,000 varieties of tomato. They come in many colours including pink, purple, black, yellow and white.

This low-calorie super-green soup is a good lunch option after an overly indulgent weekend as it is light and packed full of nutrients.

WATERCRESS AND BROCCOLI SOUP

SERVES 2
Vegetarian and *Dairy-free*

PREP TIME
10 minutes

COOK TIME
2 hours on high

INGREDIENTS
1 head of broccoli, chopped
1 small onion, peeled and diced
1 small potato, peeled and diced
85g watercress
1 garlic clove, crushed
sea salt and black pepper
yoghurt and snipped chives,
   to serve (optional)

A little dollop of yoghurt makes this soup nice and creamy and it helps to balance out the peppery taste of the watercress.

Watercress is a massively underrated green leaf in my opinion and this is a great way to get the most out of it. It might be 95 per cent water, but it has a lot of flavour.

1 Preheat your slow cooker to high.
2 Put the broccoli, onion, potato, watercress, garlic and 500ml water in the slow cooker and cook for 2 hours.
3 Use a hand blender to blend until smooth, then season to taste. Divide between bowls and serve with a drizzle of yoghurt and a sprinkle of chives, if wished.

NUTRITIONAL FACT
Watercress is one of the lowest-calorie foods, with only 11 calories per 100g.

A thick Italian soup with so many ingredients in it that there really is something for everyone. Minestrone is about as filling and comforting as soup gets, and do not be put off by lots of different ingredients, as this is a budget-friendly soup.

MINESTRONE SOUP

SERVES 4
Vegan

PREP TIME
10 minutes

COOK TIME
2½ hours on high

INGREDIENTS
1 x 400g can chopped tomatoes
1 x 400g can cannellini beans
750ml vegetable stock
2 tbsp tomato purée
2 carrots, peeled and diced
1 courgette, diced
1 celery stick, diced
2 garlic cloves, crushed
1 onion, diced
2 tbsp dried oregano
1 tbsp dried marjoram
60g small pasta pieces
¼ head of green cabbage,
   shredded
sea salt and black pepper

This chunky soup does not need any bread with it, as it is filled out with pasta. It is a go-to when you are feeling unwell and need a pick-me-up, and is the perfect meal for a chilly night.

1 Preheat your slow cooker to high.
2 Put the tomatoes, beans, stock, tomato purée, carrots, courgette, celery, garlic, onion, oregano and marjoram in the slow cooker and cook for 2 hours.
3 Add the pasta and cabbage and cook for a further 30 minutes, or until the pasta is tender. Season to taste and serve.

NUTRITIONAL FACT
Cabbage is high in dietary fibre, vitamins A, B6, C and K, folate, potassium, manganese, thiamin, calcium, iron and magnesium.

I call this a super-green summer soup because, let's face it, in the UK we have a lot of soup weather in the summer, and this is a great way to use summer asparagus in a warming meal.

SPINACH AND ASPARAGUS SOUP

SERVES 4
Vegan

PREP TIME
10 minutes

COOK TIME
4 hours on high

INGREDIENTS
200g asparagus, chopped
250g potato, peeled and chopped
5 shallots, diced
3 garlic cloves, crushed
500ml vegetable stock
juice and zest of ½ a lemon
150g spinach
½ pack of fresh chives,
    finely chopped
sea salt and black pepper

The shallots make a flavourful base for the soup and it is a delicious starter to a heavier main. This is a budget-friendly soup that will give you a pick-me-up on a drab summer day.

1 Preheat your slow cooker to high.
2 Put the asparagus, potato, shallots, garlic and stock in the slow cooker and cook for 4 hours.
3 Add the lemon juice, spinach and chives and use a hand blender to blend until smooth. Season to taste and serve.

NUTRITIONAL FACT
100g of spinach contains about 25 per cent of the recommended daily intake of iron, one of the highest for any green leafy vegetable.

Main meals

POULTRY

24 delicious recipes including:

Jerk Chicken

Sun-dried Tomato and
Basil Turkey Meatballs

Chicken Fajitas

Asian Chicken Lettuce Wraps

Vietnamese-style Chicken
with Pak Choi

Butternut Squash and
Apple Sausage Casserole

Chicken and Courgette Pasta 'Bake'

Jambalaya

Chicken Teriyaki Bowls

and

Greek Chicken Flatbreads

Switch up your lunchtime routine and try wraps instead of sandwiches. Lean turkey cooked in a tangy homemade BBQ sauce and served in wraps with creamy avocado will liven up any lunchbox or picnic.

BBQ TURKEY AND AVOCADO WRAPS

SERVES 4
Kid-approved

PREP TIME
15 minutes

COOK TIME
4 hours on high plus 10 minutes

INGREDIENTS
1 tbsp olive oil
1 onion, diced
2 garlic cloves, crushed
500g carton of passata
1 tbsp paprika
2 tbsp maple syrup
2 tbsp balsamic vinegar
1 tbsp Worcestershire sauce
4 small turkey steaks (about 100g each), cut into small chunks

To serve

½ romaine lettuce, shredded
2 tomatoes, diced
1 avocado, mashed
2 wraps

You can get some super-thin wraps that will save you some calories too. What makes this a healthier lunchtime option is the homemade BBQ sauce, as you can control the sweetness. This recipe only uses half the BBQ sauce that you will make, but I am sure you will not have any trouble finding uses for the leftovers. If you need inspiration, use it as a dip for the garlic potato wedges (page 180).

1 Preheat your slow cooker to high.
2 Put the oil in a saucepan, add the onion and garlic and gently cook for 3 minutes. Add the passata, paprika, maple syrup, balsamic vinegar and Worcestershire sauce and mix well. Simmer for 5 minutes, then put in a blender and blend until smooth. This is the barbecue sauce.
3 Put the turkey steaks in the slow cooker and add half of the barbecue sauce on top (the rest can keep in the fridge for 4 days). Cook for 4 hours. Once it is cooked, use two forks to shred the meat and mix well with the sauce.
4 Divide the lettuce, tomato and avocado between the wraps and top with the cooked BBQ turkey. Wrap up and serve.

NUTRITIONAL FACT
Avocados contain 4 per cent protein, making them the fruit with the highest protein content.

You can almost imagine you are sunning yourself in Jamaica whilst eating this jerk chicken with rice 'n' peas. Not for the faint hearted, this jerk sauce has a serious kick, but you can add less chilli if you prefer things on the milder side.

JERK CHICKEN

SERVES 2

PREP TIME
15 minutes

COOK TIME
4 hours on high

INGREDIENTS
4 tbsp olive oil
juice of 1 lime
a thumb-sized piece of ginger
4 spring onions
2 Scotch bonnets
    (or less for less heat)
1 tbsp mustard seeds
½ tsp salt
1 tbsp peppercorns
2 tbsp white wine vinegar
2 garlic cloves
1 tbsp dried thyme
2 tbsp tomato purée
1 tbsp brown sugar or honey
4 tbsp rum (optional, but it tastes
    even better this way)
1 tbsp ground allspice
1 tsp cayenne
2 chicken breasts, diced into
    chunks

To serve

120g rice
1 x 400g can pinto beans, drained
    and rinsed
juice of 1 lime juice

Slow cooking the chicken in the jerk sauce makes it really nice and succulent, and although this recipe uses chicken breasts to keep it leaner, you could use thighs for even more flavour – just note that cooking times could then vary.

1 Preheat your slow cooker to high.
2 Put all the ingredients except the chicken in a food processor and blend until smooth. If you do not have one, then use a pestle and mortar to pound them into a paste.
3 Put the chicken chunks into your slow cooker. Pour over the jerk sauce and add 100ml water. Put the lid on and cook in the slow cooker for 4 hours until the chicken is cooked through and tender.
4 Meanwhile, cook the rice according to the packet instructions. Drain and mix it with the beans and lime juice.
5 Serve the jerk chicken with the rice.

FUN FACT
Most Scotch bonnets have a heat rating of 100,000–350,000 Scoville units. For comparison, most jalapeño peppers are 2,500 to 8,000 on the Scoville heat scale.

Sun-dried tomatoes are a great way to add a big burst of flavour without adding a lot of extra calories, and these sun-dried tomato and basil turkey meatballs are almost guaranteed to be your new go-to for spaghetti and meatballs night.

SUN-DRIED TOMATO AND BASIL TURKEY MEATBALLS

SERVES 4
Freezer-friendly and *Kid-approved*

PREP TIME
20 minutes

COOK TIME
6 hours on low, plus 5 minutes

INGREDIENTS

For the meatballs

2 slices of wholemeal bread
500g lean turkey breast mince
1 small egg
20g grated Parmesan cheese
2 tbsp dried basil
2 garlic cloves, crushed
8 sun-dried tomatoes in oil,
   drained and chopped
1 tbsp olive oil
sea salt and black pepper

For the sauce

1 x 400g can chopped tomatoes
1 small onion, finely diced
2 tbsp sun-dried tomato paste
2 garlic cloves, crushed
a handful of fresh basil leaves

Although meatballs are traditionally made with beef or pork (or a mixture), using turkey mince makes them a bit leaner and gives a nice change of flavour.

1 Preheat your slow cooker to low.
2 Put the bread slices in a blender and blitz until you have breadcrumbs. Put in a large bowl and add the turkey mince, egg (add half at a time in case the mixture becomes too wet), Parmesan, dried basil, garlic, sun-dried tomatoes and some seasoning. Mix well using your hands, then roll into 12 meatballs.
3 Heat the oil in a large frying pan over medium heat and brown the meatballs for 2–3 minutes, turning often.
4 For the sauce, put the chopped tomatoes, onion, sun-dried tomato paste and garlic in the slow cooker and mix well. Gently add the meatballs and cook for 6 hours until the meatballs are cooked through.
5 Stir through the fresh basil before serving on a bed of pasta.

NUTRITIONAL FACT
Per portion, turkey meat contains more protein per gram than beef, pork and chicken.

Store-bought teriyaki sauce is usually packed with sugar and overly sweet, but making your own lighter version is really easy and you can control the sweetness.

CHICKEN TERIYAKI BOWLS

SERVES 4
Freezer-friendly

PREP TIME
10 minutes

COOK TIME
8 hours on low

INGREDIENTS
2 chicken breasts
4 shallots, peeled and diced
4 carrots, peeled and cut into
  sticks
2 tbsp honey
2 tbsp soy sauce
2 garlic cloves, crushed
2 tbsp finely grated fresh ginger
juice of ½ a lime
125ml chicken stock
1 head of broccoli, chopped
  into florets

To serve

cooked rice
4 pineapple rings, cut into chunks
sesame seeds, to sprinkle

These chicken teriyaki bowls are topped with crunchy vegetables and make a lighter alternative to ordering a takeaway. This sweet and salty chicken is so simple it will become a regular on your weekly meal planner.

1 Preheat your slow cooker to low.
2 Put the chicken, shallots and carrots in the slow cooker.
3 In a separate bowl, mix together the honey, soy sauce, garlic, ginger, lime juice and stock. Pour over the chicken and cook for 8 hours.
4 Thirty minutes before it is ready, add the broccoli and continue cooking.
5 Take the chicken out of the slow cooker and shred with two forks. Put it back into the slow cooker and mix well.
6 Serve the chicken and vegetables in bowls on rice, scattered with pineapple chunks and sesame seeds.

With minimal effort and just one main ingredient (if you do not include the seasoning), you have the base of so many different meals to see you through the week.

WHOLE SLOW-COOKED CHICKEN

SERVES 8

PREP TIME
5 minutes

COOK TIME
4 hours on high

INGREDIENTS
1 medium chicken
1 tsp garlic powder
1 tsp onion powder
1 tsp ground cumin
1 tsp paprika
sea salt and black pepper

We cook this on a Sunday afternoon to have with a roast dinner, and then the leftovers get shredded up to go on salads and in sandwiches, curries and noodle dishes for quick and easy meals at the end of a busy day.

1 Preheat your slow cooker to high.
2 Roll some kitchen foil into 3 balls and put them in the bottom of the slow cooker. Put the chicken on top.
3 Put the garlic powder, onion powder, cumin, paprika and a pinch of salt and pepper in a bowl and mix together. Once combined, sprinkle over the chicken and rub it in.
4 Cook for 3½–4 hours until cooked through.

TOP TIPS
If anyone in your family is a fan of the chicken skin (admittedly, not the healthiest part), then after the chicken has finished cooking in the slow cooker, transfer the skin to a baking tray and put under the grill for 2–3 minutes until it crisps up.

Do not get rid of the liquid at the bottom of the slow cooker – use it to make stock to add to some of the soups in this book.

I am a big fan of lettuce wraps. They are a lower-carb alternative to flour wraps, so you can pile up all the toppings – and let's face it, it's all about the toppings anyway.

ASIAN CHICKEN LETTUCE WRAPS

SERVES 4

PREP TIME
10 minutes

COOK TIME
2 hours on high, plus 5 minutes

INGREDIENTS
2 large chicken breasts,
    roughly chopped
1 tsp olive oil
1 small onion, diced
200ml chicken stock
juice of 1 lime
1 tbsp Chinese 5 spice
2 tbsp soy sauce
1 tbsp garlic powder
1 tsp ground ginger
4 handfuls of shredded carrot
    and cabbage
8 little gem lettuce leaves
4 spring onions, chopped
hot sauce (optional)
red chillies, sliced (optional)

These are kind of like an Asian version of fajitas and they are high in protein, too.

You could easily put the filling on top of noodles or rice, though, if you want something a bit more filling.

1 Preheat your slow cooker to high.
2 Put the chicken breasts in a food processor and blend until they become mince.
3 Heat the oil in a frying pan over medium heat, then add the ground chicken breast and onion and cook for about 3 minutes, or until no longer pink. Use a wooden spoon to separate the chunks into small pieces as the chicken cooks.
4 Put the chicken and onion in a slow cooker with the chicken stock, lime juice, Chinese 5 spice, soy sauce, garlic powder and ground ginger and cook for 2 hours.
5 Divide the shredded carrot and cabbage between the little gem leaves, then use a slotted spoon to transfer the chicken from the slow cooker to the lettuce cups. Top with spring onions, and chilli sauce and chillies if using.

CHANGE IT UP
If you want to give it a creamy and nutty twist, stir in a spoonful of homemade peanut or cashew butter before cooking.

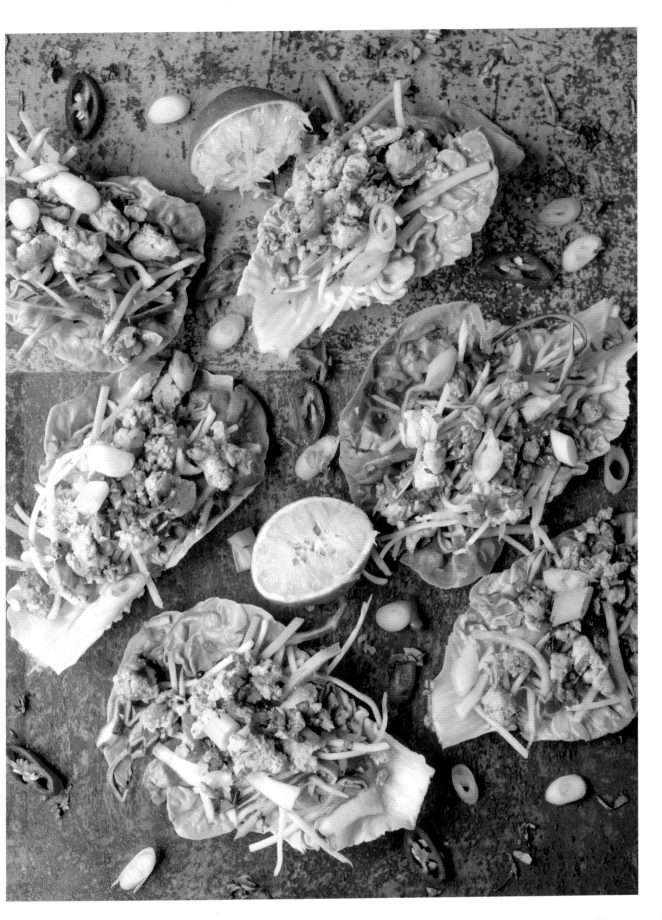

This Vietnamese-inspired chicken dish is an easy way to take a simple weeknight meal up a notch in the flavour department.

VIETNAMESE-STYLE CHICKEN WITH PAK CHOI

SERVES 4
Freezer-friendly

PREP TIME
10 minutes

COOK TIME
5 hours on low

INGREDIENTS
4 skinless, boneless chicken thighs
1 large carrot, diced
6 shallots, diced
2 tbsp soy sauce
2 tbsp fish sauce
2 tbsp sesame oil
1 tbsp honey
½ tsp crushed chilli flakes
3 garlic cloves, crushed
a thumb-sized piece of ginger,
    peeled and grated
1 vegetable stock cube
2 small heads of pak choi, chopped
cooked rice, to serve

This fragrant dish has super-succulent chicken and a little bit of spice, and it is a real crowd-pleaser – something we have made over and over again. You could use any greens in this, but the pak choi has such a lovely texture that pairs well with the melt-in-your-mouth chicken. Vietnamese food is having a big impact on the food scene with its simple but bold flavours, and this is a good introduction to the cuisine.

1 Preheat your slow cooker to low.
2 Put the chicken thighs in the slow cooker and put the carrot and shallots on top.
3 In a bowl, mix together the soy sauce, fish sauce, sesame oil, honey, chilli flakes, garlic, ginger, stock cube and 80ml boiled water and mix well. Pour over the chicken and put the lid on the slow cooker. Cook for 5 hours.
4 Half an hour before it is ready, remove the chicken and add the pak choi to the liquid in the slow cooker. Mix well, then put the chicken back on top, put the lid back on and cook for the final 30 minutes. When ready, serve on rice.

TOP TIP
The best way to peel ginger is by using a teaspoon to scrape the skin off.

Whilst we can never get tired of a comforting chicken and potato combination, this Italian herb blend brings what could be an easily bland combination to life.

ITALIAN CHICKEN AND POTATOES

SERVES 2

PREP TIME
5 minutes

COOK TIME
7 hours on low

INGREDIENTS
10 new potatoes, halved or
   quartered depending on size
2 chicken breasts
2 tbsp olive oil
1 tsp garlic powder
1 tsp onion powder
1 tbsp dried oregano
1 tbsp dried marjoram
1 tbsp dried basil
1 tbsp dried rosemary
1 tbsp crushed chilli flakes
sea salt and black pepper
chopped fresh parsley, to serve

This is a hearty meal in one pot, but a few steamed vegetables on the side would go a long way. This is simple comfort food central!

1 Preheat your slow cooker to low.
2 Put the potatoes and chicken in a large bowl, then drizzle over the oil and sprinkle in all the seasonings. Stir well, then transfer to the slow cooker.
3 Cook for 6–7 hours, or until the chicken is cooked through and a fork easily goes through the potatoes.
4 Serve with a sprinkling of parsley.

Did you know that meatballs make a great addition to any party food table? You do not just have to serve them with spaghetti, as these sweet chilli meatballs, skewered with cocktail sticks for easy eating, will not last long at your next get-together.

SWEET CHILLI CHICKEN MEATBALLS

SERVES 4
Freezer-friendly

PREP TIME
20 minutes

COOK TIME
6 hours on low, plus 5 minutes

INGREDIENTS
For the meatballs

2 slices of wholemeal bread
2 chicken breasts
1 tbsp garlic powder
1 tbsp onion powder
1 tbsp dried oregano
1 tbsp cayenne pepper
½ tsp ground cumin
½ tsp paprika
1 small egg, whisked
1 tbsp olive oil
sea salt and black pepper

For the sauce

300ml passata
2 tbsp honey
2 garlic cloves, crushed
fresh basil, to serve

Just a hint of sweetness cuts through the spice of these lean chicken meatballs.

1 Preheat your slow cooker to low.
2 Put the bread slices in a blender and blitz until breadcrumbs form. Put to one side.
3 Put the chicken breasts in the blender and blitz until it forms a mince-like consistency.
4 In a large bowl, combine the breadcrumbs, minced chicken, garlic powder, onion powder, oregano, cayenne, cumin, paprika, some salt and pepper and the egg. Mix with your hands, then form into 12 meatballs.
5 Heat the olive oil in a large frying pan over medium heat, add the meatballs and cook for 2–3 minutes, turning regularly, until browned on all sides.
6 Add the passata, honey and garlic to the slow cooker and stir. Add the meatballs and gently stir so that they are all covered in sauce. Cook for 6 hours.
7 Sprinkle with fresh basil before serving.

BONUS RECIPE
Got any leftover meatballs? Put them in a sub roll with some of the vegetables from page 174 for a lunchtime sandwich that is far from boring.

A sausage casserole is always a warming autumn and winter favourite, but it is easy to give what can be a traditionally stodgy meal a bit of a health kick by adding some chunks of vegetables.

BUTTERNUT SQUASH AND APPLE SAUSAGE CASSEROLE

SERVES 4
Freezer-friendly and *Kid-approved*

PREP TIME
10 minutes

COOK TIME
4 hours on high, plus 5 minutes

INGREDIENTS
1 tbsp olive oil
8 lean chicken sausages
1 small butternut squash, peeled and diced
1 apple, diced
1 red onion, cut into chunks
2 garlic cloves, crushed
1 tbsp dried oregano
1 tbsp dried thyme
200ml mushroom stock
1 x 400g can chopped tomatoes
2 tbsp tomato purée
sea salt and black pepper
fresh parsley, chopped, to serve

This recipe has just two sausages per portion and is bulked out with creamy butternut squash, so you still get all of the flavour from the meat, but it's lower in fat than the standard sausage casserole. Apple and sausage go really well together and not only does the fruit add some extra sweetness, but some added texture too.

1 Preheat your slow cooker to high.
2 Add the oil to a large frying pan over medium heat. Add the sausages and cook, turning regularly, until they are brown on all sides.
3 Put the sausages in the slow cooker with the butternut squash, apple, red onion, garlic, oregano, thyme, stock, tomatoes and tomato purée and season with salt and pepper. Cook for 4 hours until the sausages are cooked through and all the vegetables are tender. Serve sprinkled with chopped fresh parsley.

TOP TIP
The best way to dice a butternut squash: cut off the ends first, then peel the skin off with a sharp peeler. Cut the squash in half at the neck (where it starts to bulge). Slice the neck into discs, then into cubes. Scoop out the seeds and slice into rings, then cubes.

One of the UK's favourite Chinese dishes, sweet and sour chicken is easy to make and this homemade sauce makes it a lighter option too.

SWEET AND SOUR CHICKEN

SERVES 4
Freezer-friendly

PREP TIME
15 minutes

COOK TIME
6 hours on low

INGREDIENTS
2 skinless chicken breasts,
   cut into chunks
1 small onion, diced
1 carrot, peeled and diced
1 red pepper, deseeded and diced
1 green pepper, deseeded and diced
2 tbsp soy sauce
2 tbsp tomato purée
2 garlic cloves, crushed
½ thumb-sized piece of ginger,
   peeled and grated
2 tbsp honey
2 tbsp apple cider vinegar
170ml chicken stock
1 x 220g can pineapple chunks,
   drained
cooked rice, to serve

What makes this recipe healthier? It is not heavy in oil and although the sauce is nice and sweet, it has less sugar than a standard sauce and the peppers and chunks of pineapple add some natural sweetness, too.

1 Preheat your slow cooker to low.
2 Put the chicken, onion, carrot and peppers in the slow cooker.
3 In a bowl, combine the soy sauce, tomato purée, garlic, ginger, honey, vinegar and stock and mix well. Pour into the slow cooker and mix everything together.
4 Cook for 5½ hours, then add the pineapple and cook for 30 minutes more, until the chicken has cooked through and the sauce has thickened a little.

CHANGE IT UP
For a lighter swap, instead of serving this on rice, try it on cauliflower 'rice' for a lower-carb version. Finely grate a head of cauliflower, or whizz it in a blender, then put it in a microwaveable dish, cover and cook for 5 minutes.

Pasta bakes are about as easy as comfort food gets, and this healthy twist has lots of courgette shredded up and hidden in it. It is a family favourite that can be easily adapted to include various squash or greens.

CHICKEN AND COURGETTE PASTA 'BAKE'

SERVES 4
Freezer-friendly and *Kid-approved*

PREP TIME
20 minutes

COOK TIME
4 hours and 15 minutes on high

INGREDIENTS
2 chicken breasts
1 courgette
2 x 400g cans chopped tomatoes
3 garlic cloves, crushed
2 tbsp dried oregano
20 fresh basil leaves, finely
    chopped, plus extra to serve
240g dried penne pasta
60g mature cheese
sea salt and black pepper

1 Preheat your slow cooker to high.

2 Put the chicken breasts in the slow cooker and season with some salt and pepper.

3 Grate the courgette, then squeeze out all the excess liquid and add the courgette to the slow cooker.

4 Add the chopped tomatoes, garlic, oregano and basil and stir well. Cook for 4 hours.

5 Meanwhile, put the pasta in a pan of boiling water and cook according to packet instructions, then drain.

6 Once the chicken has cooked for 4 hours, shred it with two forks, then add the drained pasta to the slow cooker and stir in. Sprinkle the cheese over the top, put the lid back on and cook for a further 15 minutes, or until the cheese melts.

7 Serve with a sprinkle of fresh basil.

Just a few simple ingredients and say goodbye to dry chicken and hello to moist lemony and garlic chicken. Serve with pasta, on a salad or with some potatoes and vegetables.

LEMON AND GARLIC CHICKEN BREASTS

SERVES 4

PREP TIME
5 minutes

COOK TIME
3 hours on high

INGREDIENTS
4 chicken breasts
120ml chicken stock
juice and grated zest of 1 lemon
3 garlic cloves, crushed
2 tbsp olive oil
1 tbsp dried oregano
sea salt and black pepper
fresh parsley, chopped, to serve

1 Preheat your slow cooker to high.
2 Put the chicken breasts in the slow cooker and season with salt and pepper.
3 Mix the stock, lemon juice and zest, garlic, oil and oregano together in a bowl and pour over the chicken.
4 Cook for 3 hours until the chicken is cooked through. Serve sprinkled with chopped fresh parsley.

TOP TIP
The best way to peel garlic is to place the flat side of a chef's knife over the garlic clove. Press with your palm to smash the clove quickly and carefully. Remove the knife and finish the peeling process by hand.

This Louisiana classic is smoky with a hint of spice. It is like a creole version of paella and is lean and full of flavour.

JAMBALAYA

SERVES 2

PREP TIME
10 minutes

COOK TIME
4 hours on high, plus 5 minutes

INGREDIENTS
1 tbsp olive oil
1 onion, diced
2 celery sticks, diced
1 green pepper, deseeded and diced
3 garlic cloves, crushed
2 chicken breasts, cut into chunks
2 lean chicken sausages, sliced
1 x 400g can chopped tomatoes
250ml chicken stock
2 tbsp tomato purée
1 tbsp dried oregano
1 tbsp dried thyme
1 tsp smoked paprika
1 tsp cayenne pepper (or to taste)
165g brown rice
sea salt and black pepper
sliced spring onions, to serve

1 Preheat your slow cooker to high.
2 Heat the olive oil in a large frying pan over medium heat, add the onion, celery, green pepper and garlic and cook gently for 2 minutes.
3 Add the chicken and sausage and cook for a further 2 minutes until browned.
4 Put the mixture into the slow cooker and add the chopped tomatoes, stock, tomato purée, oregano, thyme, paprika and cayenne and season with salt and pepper. Stir, then cook for 3½ hours.
5 Stir the rice into the mixture and cook for a further 30 minutes.
6 Serve with spring onions sprinkled on top.

FUN FACT
In Cajun cooking, the use of onions, sweet peppers and celery is known as 'The Holy Trinity'.

If you are looking for a lower-carb version of a burrito, then give these burrito bowls a try – all the flavour, but fewer calories. You can put all the different elements of the dish in separate bowls on the table and let everyone build their own bowl.

CHICKEN BURRITO BOWLS

SERVES 4
Freezer-friendly – without toppings

PREP TIME
20 minutes

COOK TIME
4 hours on high

INGREDIENTS
1 large chicken breast
1 x 400g can chopped tomatoes
3 tbsp chipotle paste
½ tsp ground cumin
½ tsp paprika
½ tsp dried oregano
80g brown rice
60ml chicken stock
½ x 400g can black beans, drained and rinsed
1 iceberg lettuce, shredded
2 avocados, stoned and peeled
40g light feta, crumbled
sea salt and black pepper
1 recipe quantity Salsa (see page 203)

1 Preheat your slow cooker to high.

2 Season the chicken breast with salt and pepper, put it in the slow cooker with the chopped tomatoes, chipotle paste, cumin, paprika and oregano and mix well. Cook for 2 hours.

3 Add the brown rice, chicken stock and black beans, stir again and cook for a further 2 hours.

4 Divide the shredded lettuce between 4 bowls. In another bowl, mash the avocados. Divide the tomato salsa and mashed avocado between the lettuce bowls.

5 Once the chicken is cooked, use two forks to shred it and mix everything in the slow cooker together. Divide it between the salad bowls and serve with a sprinkling of feta on top.

FUN FACT
Jalapeños were the first peppers that travelled into space on a NASA shuttle in 1982.

Burgers do not have to just be fast food; they can be a slow and healthy food too. Make burger night a little bit leaner by making your own turkey burgers.

TURKEY BURGERS

SERVES 4
Freezer-friendly and *Kid-approved*

PREP TIME
15 minutes

COOK TIME
3 hours on high

INGREDIENTS
2 slices of wholemeal bread
400g lean turkey mince
1 egg, beaten
2 garlic cloves, crushed
2 tbsp Worcestershire sauce
4 tbsp finely chopped fresh
  parsley
½ tsp ground cumin
½ tsp paprika
sea salt and black pepper

To serve

wholemeal buns
lettuce
tomatoes
BBQ sauce (page 50)

Turkey burgers can sometimes be a little dry, but slow cooking them keeps them nice and moist.

1 Preheat your slow cooker to high.
2 Put the bread slices in a food processor and blitz to make breadcrumbs.
3 Put the turkey mince in a large bowl with the breadcrumbs and beaten egg and mix well.
4 Add the garlic, Worcestershire sauce, parsley, cumin, paprika and salt and pepper. Combine well, then form into four burger patties.
5 Roll up balls of kitchen foil and put them at the bottom of the slow cooker, so the burgers can sit on them. Sit the burgers on the foil balls and cook for 3 hours, or until cooked through.
6 Serve in buns with lettuce, tomato and BBQ or your sauce of choice.

The smell of this coming out of your kitchen will almost make you believe that you are sitting in a restaurant in Barcelona. Tender chunks of smoky paprika chicken and just enough chorizo add a ton of flavour but not a lot of extra calories.

SPANISH CHICKEN

SERVES 4

PREP TIME
10 minutes

COOK TIME
8 hours on low, plus 5 minutes

INGREDIENTS
3 chicken breasts, cut into chunks
1 tbsp olive oil
2 tsp paprika
100g chorizo, diced
1 small onion, diced
1 red pepper, roughly chopped
1 green pepper, roughly chopped
4 garlic cloves, chopped
200ml vegetable stock
1 x 400g can chopped tomatoes
2 tbsp tomato purée
2 tbsp dried oregano
1x 400g can butter beans, drained
10 mixed pitted olives, halved
sea salt and black pepper

1 Preheat your slow cooker to low.

2 Place the chicken, olive oil and paprika in a zip lock bag, season with and salt and pepper and shake well.

3 Heat a large non-stick frying pan over medium heat, add the chicken, chorizo, onion and peppers and gently cook until the chicken has browned (around 3–4 minutes).

4 Put the chicken mixture in the slow cooker with the garlic, stock, tomatoes, tomato purée, oregano, beans and olives.

5 Cook for 8 hours, or until the chicken is cooked through.

We learnt how to make traditional Thai red curry – including making the paste from scratch – at a cookery school when we were travelling around Thailand, and this is my adapted slow cooker version.

THAI RED CHICKEN CURRY

SERVES 4
Freezer-friendly

PREP TIME
10 minutes

COOK TIME
3 hours on high

INGREDIENTS
1 large shallot, roughly chopped
1 small red chilli (or more or
    less, depending on how spicy
    you like it)
1 tbsp tomato purée
1 lemongrass stalk, bashed and
    chopped
a thumb-sized piece of ginger,
    peeled and sliced
4 garlic cloves, peeled
½ tsp ground cumin
½ tsp ground coriander
juice of 1 lime
2 tbsp soy sauce
1 x 400ml can coconut milk
    (not light)
4 chicken breasts, cut into chunks
cooked rice, to serve
fresh coriander, chopped, to serve

The creamy, spicy and fragrant sauce is worth making yourself, and after seeing how easy this is, you will never go back to a jar. Forget ordering a takeaway – just a little bit of preparation and this can be ready by the time you get home from work on a Friday night.

1 Preheat your slow cooker to high.
2 To a small food processor, add the shallot, chilli, tomato purée, lemongrass, ginger, garlic, cumin, coriander, lime juice and soy sauce and blend to make a paste.
3 Put the paste in the slow cooker with the coconut milk and mix well. Add the chicken and cook for 3 hours until the chicken is cooked through and tender.
4 Serve with rice and sprinkle with fresh coriander.

TOP TIP
To get the most flavour out of lemongrass, trim off the ends and remove and discard the first few outer layers, then bruise the lemongrass stalk by lightly crushing it with a pestle, or the blunt edge of a large knife.

A chicken korma is one of the UK's favourite curry dishes. Originating from northern Indian, it has a Persian influence and although there are various ways of cooking it, it is always creamy and fragrant.

CHICKEN KORMA

SERVES 2
Freezer-friendly

PREP TIME
10 minutes

COOK TIME
6 hours on low, plus 6 minutes

INGREDIENTS
1 tsp ground cumin
1 tsp garam masala
½ tsp paprika
1 tsp ground coriander
1 tsp ground turmeric
½ tsp chilli powder
1 tbsp olive oil
1 onion, peeled and diced
2 garlic cloves, crushed
200ml coconut milk (not light)
1 large chicken breast,
    cut into chunks
sea salt and black pepper

To serve

cooked rice
desiccated coconut
flaked almonds

A rich and creamy chicken curry is not something you would usually associate with healthy eating, but this curry is lighter than most, and still with all the flavour and a hint of spice. Kormas should not be overly spicy, but you could always bump up the amount of chilli used.

1 Preheat your slow cooker to low.
2 In a bowl, combine the cumin, garam masala, paprika, coriander, turmeric, chilli powder, some salt and pepper and 4 tbsp water and mix to form a paste. You may need to add a little more water.
3 Heat the olive oil in a large frying pan over medium heat, add the onion and cook for 4 minutes. Add the garlic and the spice paste and stir well, cooking for a further 2 minutes.
4 Put the onion mixture in the slow cooker with the coconut milk and stir. Add the chicken and stir well. Cook for 6 hours until the chicken is cooked through and tender.
5 Serve with rice and a sprinkle of desiccated coconut and flaked almonds.

NUTRITIONAL FACT
This recipe uses plenty of turmeric, which is an anti-inflammatory and antioxidant. It has long been used in alternative medicine, as well as being an essential ingredient in many Asian dishes.

Creamy coconut chicken breasts with chunks of crunchy vegetables – this dish will rival any takeaway and it is much cheaper too! You can serve this on rice or noodles, or in a wrap with crunchy slaw for a leftovers lunch.

CREAMY COCONUT CHICKEN

SERVES 4
Freezer-friendly

PREP TIME
5 minutes

COOK TIME
4 hours on high

INGREDIENTS
200ml coconut milk (not light)
2 tbsp soy sauce
juice and zest of ½ a lime
2 garlic cloves, crushed
½ thumb-sized piece of ginger, grated
1 tbsp curry powder
4 tbsp finely chopped fresh coriander, plus extra to serve
3 large chicken breasts
1 carrot, peeled and diced
1 celery stick, diced
4 shallots, diced

1 Preheat your slow cooker to high.
2 Put the coconut milk, soy sauce, lime juice and zest, garlic, ginger, curry powder and coriander in a bowl and mix well.
3 Put the chicken, carrot, celery and shallots in the slow cooker and pour the coconut mixture over it.
4 Cook for 4 hours until the chicken is cooked through and tender. Serve sprinkled with fresh coriander.

FUN FACT
Coconut is a drupe, not a nut. It is related to other drupes including peaches, plums and cherries.

In my opinion, one of the best flavour combinations is balsamic vinegar, tomato and basil, and they are the key ingredients in this balsamic chicken dish. It is fresh, light and summery, and can be served with spaghetti, rice or on a salad.

BALSAMIC CHICKEN

SERVES 4
Freezer-friendly

PREP TIME
5 minutes

COOK TIME
6 hours on low

INGREDIENTS
1 red onion, thinly sliced
4 chicken breasts
    (about 500g total weight)
1 tbsp olive oil
6 tomatoes, diced
2 garlic cloves, crushed
8 basil leaves, chopped
60ml balsamic vinegar
50ml chicken stock
sea salt and black pepper

If you are in the mood for Italian, but you do not want a heavy sauce, then this zesty dish is a nice alternative. This will soon be a regular on your dinner table.

1 Preheat your slow cooker to low.
2 Put the sliced onion at the bottom of the slow cooker, then put the chicken breasts on top. Add the olive oil and season with salt and pepper.
3 Add the tomatoes, garlic and basil, then pour the balsamic vinegar and stock over the top.
4 Cook for 6 hours until the chicken is cooked and tender.

TOP TIP
As balsamic vinegar is the star of this dish, a good-quality balsamic will give the best results, so try to get the best one you can afford.

BONUS RECIPE
Got some leftover chicken? Shred it up and put in a wrap with lettuce and some feta cheese.

This is one of my favourite recipes in the book because it is the ultimate dump and leave dinner. Chicken fajitas are a weekly thing in our house and they became so much easier when we started making them in the slow cooker.

CHICKEN FAJITAS

SERVES 4
Freezer-friendly

PREP TIME
10 minutes

COOK TIME
3 hours on high

INGREDIENTS
3 chicken breasts, cut into strips
1 tbsp chilli powder (less if you do
   not want much heat)
1 tsp ground cumin
1 tsp paprika
2 red peppers, deseeded and
   cut into strips
1 yellow pepper, deseeded and
   cut in to strips
1 onion, thinly sliced
1 x 400g can chopped tomatoes
juice of ½ a lime
2 garlic cloves, crushed
sea salt and black pepper

To serve

8 tortillas
1 recipe quantity Salsa (page 203)
guacamole
grated Cheddar cheese
Greek yoghurt
fresh coriander

Although chicken fajitas are quick to make when they are sizzling on the stove, they are quite hands-on to cook whereas the slow cooker handles all that for you. So although it takes a bit longer in the slow cooker, they can be left unattended and you are free to get on with other things. Fajitas are a good way to include some vegetables in your dinner, too, and the peppers in this remain fairly crunchy with plenty of texture.

1 Preheat your slow cooker to high.
2 Place the chicken in a bowl with the chilli powder, cumin, paprika and some salt and pepper and mix well.
3 Transfer the chicken to the slow cooker and add the peppers, onion, chopped tomatoes, lime and garlic and mix well. Cook for 3 hours, until the chicken is cooked through and tender.
4 Serve the chicken in tortillas with your choice of toppings.

These chicken burgers just scream summer garden party, and your guests will be begging you for the recipe once tasted.

CHIPOTLE PULLED CHICKEN BURGERS WITH HOMEMADE SLAW

SERVES 4
Freezer-friendly and *Kid-approved*

PREP TIME
20 minutes

COOK TIME
4 hours on high

INGREDIENTS
2 chicken breasts
225g passata
2 tbsp chipotle paste
    (or 2 chipotles in adobo, chopped)
2 tbsp honey
½ tsp paprika
½ tsp ground cumin
1 tsp garlic powder
1 tsp onion powder
½ tsp ground coriander
sea salt and black pepper
wholewheat buns, to serve

For the Slaw

2 carrots, peeled and grated
1 red onion, finely sliced
½ small head of white cabbage, shredded
4 tbsp Greek yoghurt
2 tbsp apple cider vinegar
1 tbsp Dijon mustard

These burgers are deceptively easy to make – once the chicken is cooked and shredded, just put it on the table with some buns and slaw and let your guests build their own burgers. They will make a bit of a mess when eating them, but that is all part of the fun and I'm a firm believer that the messier the food is to eat, the better it tastes.

1 Preheat your slow cooker to high.
2 Put the chicken, passata, chipotle paste, honey, paprika, cumin, garlic powder, onion powder, ground coriander and some salt and pepper in the slow cooker and mix well. Cook for 4 hours.
3 Meanwhile, make the slaw by combining all the ingredients in a large bowl.
4 Once the 4 hours are up, shred the chicken using two forks and stir it into the sauce in the slow cooker.
5 Serve the pulled chicken in buns with homemade slaw.

FUN FACT
Chipotle peppers are smoked, dried jalapeño peppers.

Gyros are a snack or mealtime staple in Greece and this is slow cooker version will make all other sandwich options look a bit boring.

GREEK CHICKEN FLATBREADS

SERVES 4
Freezer-friendly and *Kid-approved*

PREP TIME
20 minutes

COOK TIME
8 hours on low

INGREDIENTS

For the chicken

2 chicken breasts
1 tbsp olive oil
2 tbsp dried oregano
1 tbsp dried mint
1 garlic clove, crushed
juice and zest of ½ a lemon
1 tbsp red wine vinegar
60ml chicken stock
1 small onion, diced
sea salt and black pepper

For the tzatziki

80g 0% fat Greek yoghurt
¼ of a cucumber, grated and
   liquid squeezed out of it
2 tbsp fresh lemon juice
2 garlic cloves, crushed
a handful of fresh mint,
   finely chopped

To serve

¼ iceberg lettuce, shredded
4 flatbreads
olives (optional)
crumbled feta (optional)
diced pepper (optional)

You'll be unable to resist this lemon and herb shredded chicken in a chunky flatbread topped with some creamy homemade tzatziki.

1 Preheat your slow cooker to low.
2 Put the chicken in a ziplock bag and pour in the olive oil, oregano, mint, garlic, lemon juice and zest and vinegar. Season with salt and pepper and shake well. Allow to marinate for a couple of hours, or overnight in the fridge.
3 Put the stock in the slow cooker with the onion and add the chicken along with all the flavourings from the bag. Cook for 6–8 hours until the chicken is cooked through.
4 Meanwhile, to make the tzatziki, put the Greek yoghurt, cucumber, lemon juice, garlic and mint in a bowl, season with salt and pepper and mix well.
5 Once the chicken is cooked, use two forks to shred the chicken, then add it back to the slow cooker and mix well.
6 Add some lettuce to a flatbread, then top with the shredded chicken and some tzatziki and any optional extra toppings.

TOP TIP
Prepare extra tzatziki as it makes a great alternative to mayonnaise in sandwiches or with chips, and you can use it as a delicious salad dressing too. If you want to give it a nutrition boost, try using courgette instead of cucumber.

Main meals

MEAT

Shepherd's Pie

Lean Beef Bolognese

Greek Lamb Pittas with Tzatziki

Sesame Beef with Broccoli

Spicy Orange Beef

Lamb Rogan Josh

Tagine-Style Lamb

Lean Beef Curry

Pulled Pork Tacos

Beef Taco Tomatoes

Sunday afternoons were not the same in our house growing up without a big pot of shepherd's pie bubbling away, and that is a tradition I fully intend to carry on.

SHEPHERD'S PIE

SERVES 4
Freezer-friendly and *Kid-approved*

PREP TIME
20 minutes

COOK TIME
4 hours on high, plus 10 minutes

INGREDIENTS
2 tbsp olive oil
1 large onion, diced
1 large carrot, diced
1 celery stick, chopped
1 green pepper, deseeded and diced
500g lean lamb mince
1 x 400g can chopped tomatoes
2 tbsp Worcestershire sauce
2 tbsp gravy granules
2 tbsp tomato purée
sea salt and black pepper

For the potato topping

3 medium potatoes, peeled and cut
  into chunks
60ml skimmed milk
1 tbsp butter (optional)

We make ours in the slow cooker, so when we come in from our Sunday afternoon walk all we need to do is top it with potatoes, and by the time we have set the table, it is ready to eat.

1 Preheat your slow cooker to high.
2 Heat the oil in a large frying pan over medium heat and fry the onion, carrot, celery and pepper until soft. Add the mince and cook until browned well.
3 Tip the mince mixture into your slow cooker and stir in the tomatoes, Worcestershire sauce, gravy granules and tomato purée, and season with salt and pepper. Cook for 3½ hours.
4 Meanwhile, boil the potatoes until soft. Drain, add the milk and butter, if using, and mash until smooth.
5 Remove the slow cooker lid and spoon off any liquid that has pooled on top of the mince. Reserve this and add it to gravy, if making.
6 Spoon the mashed potato evenly over the top of the mince and smooth level.
7 Replace the slow cooker lid and cook for a further 30 minutes until the meat mixture has cooked through.

FUN FACT
Often mistaken for each other, cottage pie and shepherd's pie are different because of the meat used. Cottage pie usually refers to a pie made with beef, whereas shepherd's pie should only be named as such if it contains lamb.

Most people's favourite family meal just got a little leaner by using lean beef mince, but less of it. Diced mushrooms are used to bulk this out, so you still get all the flavour from the meat, but it is that little bit lighter.

LEAN BEEF BOLOGNESE

SERVES 4
Freezer-friendly and *Kid-approved*

PREP TIME
10 minutes

COOK TIME
6 hours on low, plus 5 minutes

INGREDIENTS
1 tbsp olive oil
1 onion, diced
3 garlic cloves, crushed
350g lean (less than 5% fat)
   beef mince
1 large carrot, peeled and diced
10 chestnut mushrooms, diced
2 x 400g cans chopped tomatoes
4 tbsp tomato purée
1 tbsp dried oregano
1 tbsp dried marjoram
sea salt and black pepper

To serve

cooked tagliatelle
fresh basil, chopped
freshly grated Parmesan

1 Preheat your slow cooker to low.
2 Heat the oil in a frying pan set over medium heat, then add the onion and garlic and gently cook for 2 minutes. Add the beef mince and cook until browned.
3 Add the beef mixture to the slow cooker with the rest of the ingredients and cook for 5–6 hours.
4 Season to taste with salt and pepper and serve on tagliatelle with a sprinkle of fresh basil and Parmesan.

Whilst lamb is not the leanest of meats, if you trim off all the visible fat you can make a healthier version of a popular post-night-out meal.

GREEK LAMB PITTAS WITH TZATZIKI

SERVES 4
Freezer-friendly and *Kid-approved*

PREP TIME
10 minutes

COOK TIME
2 hours on high

INGREDIENTS
350g diced lamb, fat trimmed off
2 tbsp olive oil
juice and zest of 1 lemon
2 garlic cloves, crushed
2 tbsp dried oregano
sea salt and black pepper

To serve

1 recipe quantity tzatziki
  (page 95)
4 pitta breads
2 handfuls of curly lettuce
8 cherry tomatoes, halved
¼ red onion, sliced

Instead of hitting the kebab shop on your way home, put this dish on before you head out and have a healthier takeaway ready when you get back.

1 Preheat your slow cooker to high.
2 Put the lamb, olive oil, lemon juice and zest, garlic, oregano and some salt and pepper into the slow cooker and cook for 2 hours until the lamb is tender.
3 Spread tzatziki in the pocket of the pitta breads, then stuff with the lettuce, cooked lamb, tomatoes and red onion, and serve.

This is our go-to dish when we want to order a takeaway, but are trying to save some money and calories. It is the perfect Friday night dinner, with lean strips of steak and crunchy broccoli.

SESAME BEEF WITH BROCCOLI

SERVES 2
Freezer-friendly

PREP TIME
10 minutes

COOK TIME
6 hours on low, plus 5 minutes

INGREDIENTS
2 tbsp sesame oil
4 shallots, diced
a thumb-sized piece of ginger,
   peeled and finely grated
2 garlic cloves, crushed
400g braising steak, fat trimmed
   and cut into strips
250ml beef stock
60ml soy sauce
2 tbsp honey
1 head of broccoli,
   cut into chunks
2 tbsp cornflour
cooked rice, to serve
1 tbsp sesame seeds, to serve

1 Preheat your slow cooker to low.

2 Heat 1 tbsp of the sesame oil in a frying pan set over medium heat, add the shallots, ginger, garlic and braising steak and gently cook for 2 minutes until the meat is browned.

3 Add the beef mixture to the slow cooker with the stock, soy sauce, honey and the rest of the sesame oil and cook for 5½ hours.

4 Take a ladleful of liquid out of the slow cooker and put in a bowl. Whisk the cornflour into it, then add the mixture back into the slow cooker and stir in the broccoli.

5 Cook for a further 30 minutes until broccoli is cooked.

6 Serve with rice and a sprinkling of sesame seeds.

Strips of tender beef in a thick, sweet and zesty sauce is a delicious topping for chunky noodles. This dish is meant to be spicy, so it does have a bit of a kick to it, but feel free to tone it down a little and use fewer chilli flakes.

SPICY ORANGE BEEF

SERVES 2
Freezer-friendly

PREP TIME
10 minutes

COOK TIME
7¼ hours on low

INGREDIENTS
400g braising steak, cut into strips
200ml orange juice
grated zest of 1 orange
1 garlic clove, crushed
3 tbsp soy sauce
2 tbsp sesame oil
1 tbsp red chilli flakes (or more or less to taste)
1 tbsp cornflour
cooked rice noodles, to serve
sesame seeds, to serve

The combination of the spice and citrus in this dish will wake up your taste buds – and it makes a much healthier alternative to ordering dinner.

1 Preheat your slow cooker to low.
2 Put the steak, orange juice and zest, garlic, soy sauce, sesame oil and chilli flakes into the slow cooker, stir together and cook for 7 hours.
3 Remove a couple of tablespoons of the liquid, put it in a bowl with the cornflour and mix well.
4 Add the mixture back to the slow cooker, stir and cook for a further 10–15 minutes until the sauce has thickened.
5 Serve the beef with rice noodles and sesame seeds.

Rogan Josh is a takeaway favourite, but the best way to cook it, in my opinion, is in the slow cooker as it makes the chunks of lamb perfectly tender and they fall apart in your mouth.

LAMB ROGAN JOSH

SERVES 2
Freezer-friendly

PREP TIME
10 minutes

COOK TIME
8 hours on low, plus 10 minutes

INGREDIENTS
1 tbsp butter
350g lamb fillet, cut into chunks
6 shallots, diced
2 garlic cloves, crushed
½ inch piece of ginger, peeled and
    finely grated
1 tsp ground coriander
½ tsp ground turmeric
1 tsp garam masala
1 tsp ground cumin
1 tsp chilli powder
    (more if you like it spicy)
150ml vegetable stock
200g canned chopped tomatoes
4 handfuls of spinach
2 tbsp 0% fat Greek yoghurt
cooked rice or naan breads,
    to serve

This dish might be slow to cook, but it is quick to prepare and once you see how easy it is to make this rich and spice-packed sauce, you will never buy a jar of it again.

Persian in origin, and now a popular dish throughout India, this dish basically translates to 'cooked in oil at intense heat'. It is a lamb-based dish cooked in a sauce that is packed with onion, ginger, garlic, yoghurt and aromatic spices. I cannot stress enough the usefulness of having a good selection of dried herbs and spices in your kitchen, so this is the ideal opportunity to put them to good use.

1 Preheat your slow cooker to low.
2 Firstly, heat the butter in a frying pan over medium heat and add the lamb. Gently cook for a couple of minutes, until browned, then transfer to the slow cooker.
3 Put the shallots, garlic and ginger into the same pan and gently cook for 3 minutes. Add the spices, stir and cook for 1 minute, then add the stock and tomatoes and cook for 2 minutes.
4 Pour the tomato mixture over the lamb in the slow cooker. Put the lid on and cook for 8 hours until the lamb is tender. Stir through the spinach 10 minutes before the cooking time is up.
5 Before serving, stir in the Greek yoghurt and serve with rice or naan breads.

FUN FACT
There are many variants of the spice blend that goes under the name garam masala, but they all have a basic combination of cinnamon, cumin, fenugreek seeds, garlic and ginger. Other spices are added depending on the region of India in which it is made.

This Moroccan lamb stew brings all the flavour and tenderness of lamb cooked in a tagine, but is prepared in the slow cooker instead.

TAGINE-STYLE LAMB

SERVES 4
Freezer-friendly

PREP TIME
10 minutes

COOK TIME
3 hours on high, plus 5 minutes

INGREDIENTS
1 tbsp olive oil
500g diced lamb, trimmed of fat
1 onion, diced
2 carrots, diced
2 garlic cloves, crushed
2 tbsp ras-el-hanout
8 dried apricots, diced
1 x 400g can chopped tomatoes
2 tbsp tomato purée
150ml vegetable stock
1 large sweet potato, peeled
  and diced

To serve

cooked couscous
fresh coriander leaves
flaked almonds

Ras-el-hanout is a must in any spice cupboard and it is the star of this dish. The apricots and sweet potatoes add a touch of sweetness that pairs beautifully with the spices from the ras-el-hanout blend to create a dish that will warm your belly.

1 Preheat your slow cooker to high.
2 In a large frying pan, heat the oil over medium heat, then add the lamb and cook for 1 minute. Add the onion, carrot, garlic and ras-el-hanout and cook for a further 2 minutes.
3 Put the mixture in the slow cooker along with the apricots, tomatoes, tomato purée and vegetable stock and stir well. Cook for 3 hours, stirring in the sweet potato after 2 hours so that they cook in the stew for the final hour.
4 Serve the stew with couscous, sprinkled with fresh coriander and flaked almonds.

FUN FACT
The name ras el hanout is Arabic for 'head of the shop' and implies a blend of the best spices the seller has to offer.

Although a little oil has been used to brown the beef, most of the fat comes from the meat itself rather than the curry having a lot of extra fat added for flavour. The flavours of the meat and the spices shine through in this dish to make a takeaway-night winner.

LEAN BEEF CURRY

SERVES 2
Freezer-friendly

PREP TIME
10 minutes

COOK TIME
8 hours on low, plus 5 minutes

INGREDIENTS
1 tbsp olive oil
400g braising steak, trimmed of
  fat and cut into chunks
8 shallots, diced
3 garlic cloves, crushed
2.5cm piece of ginger, peeled and
  grated
1 red chilli, finely diced
1 tsp ground turmeric
1 tbsp ground cumin
1 tbsp ground coriander
1 tbsp garam masala
1 x 400g can chopped tomatoes
2 tbsp tomato purée
4 tbsp fat-free natural yoghurt
a handful of fresh coriander,
  finely chopped
cooked rice, to serve

This curry sauce is really rich and rivals most Indian takeaway offerings – and throwing it all in the slow cooker is just as easy as calling up a takeaway. This curry is one for those of you that can handle the heat.

1 Preheat your slow cooker to low.
2 Heat the oil in a frying pan over high heat, then add the steak and brown for 2–3 minutes. Transfer the steak to the slow cooker
3 Add the shallots, garlic, ginger and chilli to the frying pan and cook over a low heat for 2 minutes. Add all the spices, stir well and cook for a further 1 minute.
4 Add the shallot mixture to the slow cooker along with the chopped tomatoes and tomato purée and stir well.
5 Cook for 8 hours until the beef is tender.
6 Stir through the yoghurt and fresh coriander just before serving with rice.

CHANGE IT UP
To make it lighter you could skip the browning stage and just throw everything in the slow cooker without the oil. It would still work, but you would not get as much flavour.

The ultimate taco in my opinion, and it takes just a couple of minutes to prepare if you use leftover salsa from the recipe on page 203 in place of the chopped tomatoes and jalapeños.

PULLED PORK TACOS

SERVES 4
Freezer-friendly and *Kid-approved*

PREP TIME
10 minutes

COOK TIME
8 hours on low

INGREDIENTS
450g pork tenderloin
1 x 400g can chopped tomatoes
½ x 215g jar pickled jalapeños
  (or less for less spice)
1 tsp ground cumin
1 tsp paprika
2 garlic cloves, crushed
juice of 1 lime
sea salt and black pepper

To serve

soft tacos
homemade slaw (page 92)
diced avocado

Serve the pork in tacos with slaw or make it even lighter and serve in large lettuce leaves with extra raw vegetables. This is a great recipe for feeding a crowd.

1 Preheat your slow cooker to low.
2 Put the whole tenderloin in the slow cooker.
3 In a separate bowl, mix together the tomatoes, jalapeños, cumin, paprika, garlic, lime juice and salt and pepper, then pour it over the pork.
4 Cook for 8 hours until the pork is cooked through and tender. Shred the pork with two forks, then mix it back into the sauce.
5 Serve the pulled pork in soft tacos with homemade slaw and avocado.

These beef taco tomatoes are a low-carb option that skips the flour tortilla and uses a delicious tomato as the base.

BEEF TACO TOMATOES

SERVES 4
Freezer-friendly

PREP TIME
10 minutes

COOK TIME
3 hours on high, plus 5 minutes

INGREDIENTS
1 tbsp olive oil
500g lean (5% fat) beef mince
1 small onion, finely diced
1 red pepper, deseeded and
   finely diced
2 garlic cloves, crushed
1 tsp chilli powder
½ tsp ground cumin
1 tsp dried oregano
1 tsp paprika
200ml passata
2 tbsp tomato purée
12 large salad tomatoes
sea salt and black pepper
½ avocado, chopped into chunks,
   to serve

Best eaten using a knife and fork, rather than your hands like a regular taco, the rest of the family can have flour tortillas pilled high, whilst you can enjoy these with a salad for a lighter option. No need to make something totally different – just adapt.

1 Preheat your slow cooker to high.
2 Heat the oil in a frying pan over medium heat, add the beef mince, onion, red pepper and garlic and cook for around 2 minutes until the beef has browned.
3 Add the chilli powder, cumin, oregano, paprika, and salt and pepper to taste, and stir well.
4 Transfer to the slow cooker and stir in the passata and tomato purée. Cook for 3 hours until the beef is cooked through.
5 Cut a cross in the top of each tomato (not all the way through) and gently open them up. Top them with the cooked beef and some chunks of avocado and serve.

Main meals

FISH

Lemon and Chive Salmon

Lemon and Parsley Cod

Soy and Sesame Salmon

For this dish, you want to use a really good piece of salmon, keep the added flavours simple and let the flavour of the fish shine through. Flake the salmon up and add it to salads, pasta or sandwiches.

LEMON AND CHIVE SALMON

SERVES 4

PREP TIME
5 minutes

COOK TIME
3 hours on low

INGREDIENTS
1 piece of salmon large enough
    to just fit in the slow cooker
    (a fillet big enough for 4)
juice and zest of 1 lemon, plus
    extra lemon slices to serve
2 tbsp fresh chives, plus extra
    to serve
sea salt and black pepper

1 Preheat your slow cooker to low.

2 Put a piece of baking paper in the slow cooker (this will make it easier to take the salmon out without breaking) and lay the salmon on top of it.

3 Add the lemon juice and zest and chives on top of the salmon and season with salt and pepper.

4 Add just enough water to come up level with the top of the salmon. Cook for 2–3 hours until the fish is cooked through.

5 Serve with extra lemon juice, lemon slices and chives on top.

FUN FACT
Chives are part of the lily family and are related to onions, garlic and leeks.

Fish is much easier to cook than most people think and it does not get much simpler than this three-ingredient dish. The delicate flavour of cod does not need anything more than some lemon and parsley for a light and fresh meal.

LEMON AND PARSLEY COD

SERVES 2

PREP TIME
5 minutes

COOK TIME
2 hours on low

INGREDIENTS
2 cod fillets
juice and zest of 1 lemon
4 tbsp finely chopped fresh
    parsley
sea salt and black pepper

1 Preheat your slow cooker to low.
2 Put a sheet of baking paper in the bottom of the slow cooker and lay the cod fillets on top.
3 Squeeze the lemon juice over the cod, sprinkle the lemon zest and parsley on top and season with salt and pepper.
4 Cook for 2 hours until the fish is cooked through.

Add a ton of Asian-inspired flavour to these omega 3-rich salmon fillets with some soy sauce, and sesame seeds for a little crunch and texture. Served with rice noodles, it's the perfect meal for a busy weeknight.

SOY AND SESAME SALMON

SERVES 4

PREP TIME
5 minutes

COOK TIME
3 hours on low

INGREDIENTS
2 salmon fillets
1 tbsp sesame oil
juice of ½ a lime
2 tbsp soy sauce
1 tbsp sesame seeds

1 Preheat your slow cooker to low.

2 Put a sheet of baking paper in the bottom of the slow cooker and lay the salmon fillets on top.

3 In a bowl, mix together the sesame oil, lime juice, soy sauce and sesame seeds, then pour over the salmon.

4 Cook for 2–3 hours until the fish is cooked through.

Main meals

VEGETARIAN

27 scrummy dishes including:

Slow Cooker Sweet Potatoes 4 Ways

Three-bean Nachos

Creamy Cauliflower Spaghetti

Mediterranean Frittata

Butternut Squash Macaroni Cheese

Moroccan Chickpea Stew

Leafy Green Madras

Creamy Coconut Lentils

Spinach Gnocchi

Chipotle Black Bean Stew

Mushroom Stroganoff

White Bean and Kale Stew

Butternut Squash and Quinoa Chilli

and

'Roasted' Vegetable Salad

Lasagne is possibly the ultimate comfort food, but that does not mean you can't make it lighter and still feel like you've had a good filling meal. Slices of aubergine and courgette replace the pasta layers to make this lasagne lower in carbs and bursting with veggies.

LOW-CARB VEGGIE-PACKED LASAGNE

SERVES 4

Vegetarian, Freezer-friendly and *Kid-approved*

PREP TIME
20 minutes

COOK TIME
3 hours on high, plus 15 minutes

INGREDIENTS
3 large courgettes
1 large aubergine
1 tbsp olive oil
1 onion, diced
2 garlic cloves, crushed
1 red pepper, deseeded and diced
1 yellow pepper, deseeded and diced
10 mushrooms, sliced
500g passata
2 tbsp tomato purée
2 tbsp balsamic vinegar
a handful of fresh basil, finely chopped
50g Cheddar cheese, grated
30g Parmesan cheese, grated
cooking oil spray
sea salt and black pepper

This is one of those recipes to make after you have had an indulgent weekend, to give you a good boost of vitamins and beat the bloat.

1 Preheat your slow cooker to high.

2 Slice 2 of the courgettes and the aubergine thinly lengthways. Cut the other courgette into chunks and set aside.

3 Place the strips of courgette and aubergine on a baking tray, put under the grill and cook for 4 minutes on each side. (You can skip this step, however the vegetables will create a lot of water when in the slow cooker, giving you a liquidy lasagne. You could just drain this before serving though.)

4 Put the oil in a large frying pan set over medium heat and add the onion, garlic, peppers, mushrooms and courgette chunks. Gently cook for around 5 minutes, then add the passata, tomato purée, balsamic vinegar, seasoning and basil and simmer for 2 minutes.

5 Now it is time to layer your lasagne into the slow cooker. Mix together the grated cheeses. Spray a little oil in the slow cooker and put some of the vegetable mixture at the bottom, then add half of the aubergine slices and sprinkle over a third of the cheese.

6 Next add another layer of the vegetable mixture, followed by half the courgettes and another layer of cheese.

7 Then add the final layer of vegetable mixture, followed by the rest of the aubergine and courgette slices and top with the remainder of the cheese.

8 Cook for 2–3 hours until the vegetables are cooked through.

If you like your sweet potatoes soft, creamy and with a buttery texture, then cooking them in the slow cooker is the way to go.

SLOW COOKER SWEET POTATOES 4 WAYS

SERVES 4
Vegetarian and *Kid-approved*

PREP TIME
5 minutes, plus time to prepare
  your chosen topping

COOK TIME
8 hours on low

INGREDIENTS
4 medium sweet potatoes

This is such a simple and no-hassle way of cooking them and they literally melt in your mouth, which I do not find you get with cooking them in the oven. You have four healthy potato toppings to choose from here too, but feel free to switch them for your favourites for a comforting meal with little preparation.

1 Preheat your slow cooker to low.
2 Scrub the sweet potatoes, but do not dry them (the liquid from washing them is all you need to cook them with). Put them in the slow cooker and cook for 7–8 hours. Cooking time will vary depending on the size of your potatoes, but you will know they are cooked when you can stick a fork in them with little resistance.

TOPPINGS (ALL SERVE 1)

1 Creamy Mushrooms: Add a little oil to a pan, then add 6 sliced mushrooms and 1 crushed garlic clove. Gently cook for 4 minutes before taking off the hob and allowing to cool a little. Stir in 2 tbsp 0% fat crème fraîche and some chopped fresh parsley.

2 Mexican Style: In a bowl, mix together 4 tbsp Salsa (see page 203), 15g of grated Cheddar and half a diced avocado.

3 BBQ Beans: Mix together half a small can of drained cannellini beans and 2 tbsp BBQ sauce (see page 50).

4 Broccoli and Cheese: Mix 4 broccoli florets, steamed or boiled, together with 15g grated Cheddar and 2 tbsp snipped fresh chives.

NUTRITIONAL FACT

Sweet potatoes have almost twice as much fibre as white potatoes and they are a fantastic source of vitamins A and C and beta-carotene, which helps to keep your eyes healthy and supports the immune system.

BONUS RECIPE

If you're not vegetarian and have some leftover chicken to use up, try shredding it and mixing with some BBQ sauce (see page 50), then piling into the cooked sweet potatoes.

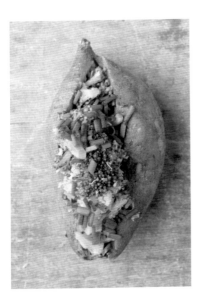  

Whether being made as a match-day dish to share, or as an easy comforting dish that you can throw together, these three-bean nachos will give you a kick of spice with a protein punch.

THREE-BEAN NACHOS

SERVES 2
Vegetarian and *Kid-approved*

PREP TIME
15 minutes

COOK TIME
2 hours on high, plus 5 minutes

INGREDIENTS
For the chilli

1 x 400g can red kidney beans, drained and rinsed

1 x 300g can pinto beans, drained and rinsed

1 x 300g can borlotti beans, drained and rinsed

1 x 400g can chopped tomatoes

1 small onion, diced

1 red pepper, deseeded and diced

2 garlic cloves, crushed

2 tbsp chipotle paste

1 tsp ground cumin

1 tsp paprika

sea salt and black pepper

To serve

300g low-salt tortilla chips

60g mature Cheddar cheese

2 spring onions, sliced

8 cherry tomatoes, halved

1 chilli, sliced

a handful of fresh coriander leaves

These are so good that you will not want to share them!

1 Preheat your slow cooker to high.

2 Put the drained beans in the slow cooker with the chopped tomatoes, onion, red pepper, garlic, chipotle, cumin, paprika and some salt and pepper.

3 Cook for 2 hours until the beans are thoroughly heated through.

4 Arrange the tortilla chips on a large plate or microwaveable/ovenproof platter, then spoon the bean chilli on top. Sprinkle the cheese over and then either put in the microwave for 90 seconds or in an oven preheated to 190ºC/Gas 5 for 5 minutes, until the cheese has melted.

5 Sprinkle the spring onions, cherry tomatoes, chilli and coriander on top and serve.

BONUS RECIPE

Even if you only need your nachos to serve two people, still cook the full amount of chilli and serve any leftover on rice for lunch the next day. You can even use the bean chilli to make a vegetarian version of the Burrito Bowls (see page 77).

If ever there was a sneaky vegetable dish, it would be this one – I have even fooled cauliflower haters with it.

CREAMY CAULIFLOWER SPAGHETTI

SERVES 2
Vegetarian and *Kid-approved*

PREP TIME
10 minutes

COOK TIME
2 hours, 40 minutes on high

INGREDIENTS
1 head of cauliflower, cut
  into chunks
500ml skimmed milk, plus extra
  if needed
125ml vegetable stock
2 garlic cloves, crushed
50g Parmesan cheese, grated
100g wholewheat spaghetti
sea salt and black pepper
a handful of fresh parsley,
  chopped, to serve

Once the cauliflower is blended with the milk, stock and cheese, it becomes a wonderfully creamy and comforting sauce that is simply paired with some spaghetti for a fuss-free cheesy pasta dish with some hidden vegetables. If you love fettuccine alfredo, then this is one for you to try.

1 Preheat your slow cooker to high.
2 Put the cauliflower, milk, stock and garlic in the slow cooker, season with salt and pepper and cook for 2 hours until the cauliflower is really tender.
3 Using a hand blender, blend until smooth. You may need to add a little more milk if it is too thick.
4 Stir in the Parmesan, then add the spaghetti (you may need to break it into shorter lengths to fit it into your slow cooker) and stir so that the sauce covers the spaghetti.
5 Cook for a further 30–40 minutes until the spaghetti is cooked. Serve sprinkled with fresh parsley.

FUN FACT
Cauliflowers aren't just available in white, but also come in many vivid colours, including orange, green and purple.

This frittata is quick to prepare and an easy lunch option that is bursting with the flavours of the Mediterranean. It is great for feeding a crowd with a big green salad on the side.

MEDITERRANEAN FRITTATA

SERVES 4
Vegetarian

PREP TIME
10 minutes

COOK TIME
2 hours on high

INGREDIENTS
8 eggs
a splash of skimmed milk
1 red pepper, deseeded and diced
10 green olives, diced
5 sun-dried tomatoes
1 small courgette, grated and the
    liquid squeezed out
4 tbsp finely chopped fresh
    parsley, plus extra to serve
80g feta cheese, crumbled
cooking oil spray
8 tomatoes on the vine
sea salt and black pepper

1 Preheat your slow cooker to high.

2 In a bowl, whisk the eggs and milk together, then add all the other ingredients, except the tomatoes on the vine, and season the mixture with salt and pepper.

3 Grease your slow cooker with a little oil and pour the egg mixture in. Gently place the tomatoes on the vine in the middle, making sure they do not sink.

4 Cook for 2 hours, or until the eggs have set. Run a knife around the edge of the slow cooker and lift the frittata out onto a large plate or board to serve sprinkled with parsley.

Stuffed peppers are the ultimate fridge-raid dinner. Almost any combination of vegetables and grains can be used as the filling, so feel free to adapt the recipe to what you have on hand. Chickpeas are added for protein, but any beans will work.

MEDITERRANEAN STUFFED PEPPERS

SERVES 2
Vegetarian and *Kid-approved*

PREP TIME
15 minutes

COOK TIME
6 hours on low

INGREDIENTS
100g couscous
200ml hot vegetable stock
1 x 400g can chopped tomatoes
3 garlic cloves, crushed
2 tbsp dried oregano
1 tbsp paprika
1 x 200g can chickpeas
4 shallots, diced
4 peppers (whatever colour
  you have)
60g light feta, crumbled
10 fresh basil leaves, finely
  chopped
sea salt and black pepper

1 Preheat your slow cooker to low.
2 Put the couscous in a large bowl, add the vegetable stock and leave for 10 minutes. Add the tomatoes, garlic, oregano, paprika, chickpeas and shallots, season with salt and pepper and mix well.
3 Slice a very thin bit off the base of the peppers (so they can stand in the slow cooker) and then slice the tops off and scoop out the insides.
4 Stuff the peppers with the couscous mixture and put them in a lightly oiled slow cooker and cook for 5½ hours.
5 Sprinkle the peppers with the feta and basil and cook for another 30 minutes until the cheese has melted and the peppers are tender.

FUN FACT
There are three main types of couscous: Moroccan, Israeli and Lebanese. This recipe uses Moroccan, the smallest of the three. Israeli couscous is bigger and Lebanese the largest.

Slow and low is the way to go when making marinara sauce. But if you don't have time to stand over the hob whilst it bubbles away, let the slow cooker do all the work for you.

PASTA MARINARA

SERVES 4

Vegetarian, Freezer-friendly and Kid-approved

PREP TIME
5 minutes

COOK TIME
8 hours on low

INGREDIENTS
2 x 400g cans good-quality
   chopped tomatoes
4 tbsp tomato purée
4 garlic cloves, crushed
1 onion, diced
1 tbsp dried marjoram
1 tbsp dried oregano
4 tbsp balsamic vinegar
2 tbsp olive oil
sea salt and black pepper

Cooking marinara over a longer period of time enhances the tomato flavour. Serve the sauce with a pasta of your choice, or use as a meatball topping.

1 Preheat your slow cooker to low.
2 Put all the ingredients in the slow cooker and cook for 8 hours.
3 You can leave it chunky, or use a hand blender to blend until smooth.

Everyone loves pasta, surely? Well, even the fussiest eaters will love this dish and I have had hundreds of comments from blog readers who have served it to vegetable-hating kids who had no idea that the sauce was bursting with vegetables.

HIDDEN VEGETABLE PASTA SAUCE

SERVES 8

Vegan, Freezer-friendly and *Kid-approved*

PREP TIME
10 minutes

COOK TIME
4 hours on high

INGREDIENTS
1 small aubergine, diced
2 peppers, deseeded and diced
2 carrots, peeled and diced
1 courgette, diced
1 leek, sliced
4 garlic cloves, crushed
2 x 400g cans chopped tomatoes
6 tbsp balsamic vinegar
200ml vegetable stock
10 basil leaves, torn
2 tbsp dried oregano
sea salt and black pepper

To serve

cooked pasta
basil leaves (optional)
shaved Parmesan (optional)

Once the sauce is blended until smooth and served with some pasta and cheese, it will look and taste like any other pasta and sauce, but with plenty of goodness hidden. This sauce is also perfect for batch cooking, as it will feed a family of four twice. So, if you are not cooking for eight, halve the sauce and put it in the freezer for another day. The Parmesan is optional – simply omit it for a vegan option.

1 Preheat your slow cooker to high.
2 Put all the sauce ingredients in your slow cooker, season with salt and pepper and cook for 4 hours until the vegetables are cooked through.
3 Blend the sauce with a hand blender until smooth, or leave chunky if you prefer.
4 Mix the sauce into the cooked pasta and serve with fresh basil and shaved Parmesan, if using.

If macaroni and cheese is your idea of comfort food, then this is a great way to sneak some extra veg into it. The butternut squash is blended into the creamy sauce, so no one would ever know.

BUTTERNUT SQUASH MACARONI CHEESE

SERVES 4

Vegetarian, Freezer-friendly and
  Kid-approved

PREP TIME
10 minutes

COOK TIME
7 hours, 40 minutes on low

INGREDIENTS
200g butternut squash cubes
2 tomatoes, diced
1 onion, diced
2 garlic cloves, crushed
350ml vegetable stock
175ml skimmed milk, plus extra
  if needed
40g mature Cheddar, grated
10 leaves of fresh basil, finely
  chopped
150g macaroni
sea salt and black pepper

1 Preheat your slow cooker to low.
2 Put the butternut squash, tomatoes, onion, garlic and stock into the slow cooker and cook for 7 hours.
3 Using a hand blender, blend the butternut squash mixture until smooth, then season with salt and pepper. Add the rest of the ingredients and mix well.
4 Cook for a further 30–40 minutes, stirring twice. You may need to add a little more milk and cook the pasta a little longer if it is still firm. It should be aldente though.
5 Serve the macaroni and cheese in bowls sprinkled with a little more black pepper.

CHANGE IT UP
You could make this vegan by using nut milk in place of the dairy and adding a little nutritional yeast instead of the cheese.

BONUS RECIPE
Don't throw away the squash seeds – simply remove the stringy bits and toast them in the oven with a little oil for a filling, healthy snack.

If you have a well-stocked spice and herb rack and a can of pulses, then you can always make a healthy and hearty meal and that is exactly what this Moroccan Chickpea Stew is.

MOROCCAN CHICKPEA STEW

SERVES 2

Vegan and *Freezer-friendly*

PREP TIME
10 minutes

COOK TIME
4 hours on high

INGREDIENTS
1 red onion, thinly sliced
1 tsp ground cumin
½ tsp paprika
2 tsp ras-el-hanout
a large handful of fresh coriander, chopped, plus extra to serve
1 x 400g can chopped tomatoes
2 tbsp tomato purée
250ml vegetable stock
40g red split lentils, rinsed
1 x 400g can chickpeas
2 tbsp harissa
4 tbsp yoghurt (vegan if wished)
sea salt and black pepper
ciabatta bread, to serve

This dish is vegan (just use coconut or soy yoghurt), budget-friendly and bursting with Moroccan flavours.

1 Preheat your slow cooker to high.
2 Add all of the ingredients except the yoghurt to the slow cooker, season with salt and pepper and cook for 4 hours.
3 Stir in the yoghurt and serve the stew with ciabatta bread and extra coriander on top.

If you like you like your curries on the spicy side, then give this Leafy Green Madras a try. If kale and spinach are not your favourite vegetables, this is a good way to introduce these mighty, iron-packed leaves into your diet.

LEAFY GREEN MADRAS

SERVES 2

Vegan and *Freezer-friendly*

PREP TIME
10 minutes

COOK TIME
4 hours on low, plus 7 minutes

INGREDIENTS
1 tbsp olive oil
1 onion, finely diced
2 garlic cloves, crushed
½ thumb-sized piece of ginger,
    peeled and grated
1 red chilli (or less for less heat),
    finely chopped
1 tbsp garam masala
½ tsp ground coriander
½ tsp ground turmeric
½ tsp ground cumin
1 x 400g can good-quality chopped
    tomatoes
2 tbsp tomato purée
150ml vegetable stock
50g curly kale, chopped
150g spinach
cooked rice, to serve
coriander leaves, to sprinkle

1 Preheat your slow cooker to low.

2 Heat the oil in a frying pan over medium heat, then add the onion and gently cook for 4 minutes. Add the garlic, ginger and chilli and cook for a further 2 minutes.

3 Add the garam masala, ground coriander, turmeric and cumin to the onion mix, stir well and cook for a further 1 minute

4 Put the onion mixture in the slow cooker with the rest of the ingredients and cook for 4 hours, until all the flavours have come together and the sauce is cooked through.

5 Serve with rice and a sprinkle of coriander.

The smell of this dish cooking is incredible and you might be tempted to walk in and out of your kitchen a few times just to let that smell hit you again.

CREAMY COCONUT LENTILS

SERVES 2

Vegan, Freezer-friendly and Kid-approved

PREP TIME
10 minutes

COOK TIME
6 hours on low

INGREDIENTS
170g red lentils, rinsed
1 onion, diced
2 garlic cloves, crushed
½ thumb-sized piece of ginger, peeled and finely grated
1 tbsp garam masala
1 tsp cayenne pepper
½ tsp ground turmeric
2 tbsp tomato purée
1 x 400g can good-quality chopped tomatoes
200ml light coconut milk
200ml vegetable stock
sea salt and black pepper
cooked rice, to serve
coriander, to serve

Fragrant coconut is the star of this dish and it is combined with protein-packed lentils for a rich and creamy meal on a budget. Try something different this meatless Monday and make a batch of this, but be sure to make extra as the leftovers are just as good.

1 Preheat your slow cooker to low.
2 Put all of the ingredients into the slow cooker, season with salt and pepper and mix well. Cook for 6 hours until the lentils are cooked and tender.
3 Serve with rice and a sprinkle of fresh coriander leaves.

FUN FACT
Lentils have been eaten by humans since Neolithic times and were one of the first domesticated crops.

Dhal makes a cheap, filling and healthy meal with protein-rich lentils, but this version has plenty of added greens that make it even more more nutritious.

SPINACH DHAL

SERVES 2
Vegan and *Freezer-friendly*

PREP TIME
10 minutes

COOK TIME
6 hours on low

INGREDIENTS
150g red lentils, rinsed
1 onion, diced
1 x 400g can tomatoes
500ml vegetable stock
3 garlic cloves, crushed
2.5cm piece of ginger,
    peeled and grated
½ tsp ground cumin
½ tsp ground turmeric
½ tsp chilli powder
a small handful of coriander,
    roughly chopped
2 handfuls of spinach
100ml light coconut milk

Any leftovers will freeze really well and are great for a quick reheated meal, served either over rice or a jacket potato or just a bigger portion by itself. Warming spices make this vegan and gluten-free dish perfect for those darker evenings when there is a chill in the air.

1 Preheat your slow cooker to low.
2 Put the lentils, onion, tomatoes, stock, garlic, ginger, cumin, turmeric and chilli powder in the slow cooker and cook for 5 hours.
3 Add the coriander, spinach and coconut milk and cook for a further 1 hour until the lentils are cooked through.

CHANGE IT UP
If you prefer more of a soup than a stew, add some extra stock once it has finished cooking for a hearty and filling soup.

One of the great things about gnocchi is that it takes just minutes to make. If you want to have it served pasta-bake style then that takes a little longer, but the slow cooker takes all the hassle out of the cooking and it is much more convenient.

SPINACH GNOCCHI

SERVES 4

Vegetarian, Freezer-friendly and *Kid-approved*

PREP TIME
5 minutes

COOK TIME
4 hours on high

INGREDIENTS
1 x 500g pack of gnocchi
2 garlic cloves, crushed
1 onion, diced
1 tbsp olive oil
2 tbsp balsamic vinegar
2 x 400g cans of tomatoes
1 tbsp dried oregano
10 fresh basil leaves, chopped
2 handfuls of spinach
40g mozzarella, shredded
sea salt and black pepper

Less than five minutes of prep time and you have yourself a thick tomatoey, iron-rich comfort dish that you could easily just eat straight out of the slow cooker.

1 Preheat your slow cooker to high.
2 Put all of the ingredients expect the spinach and mozzarella in the slow cooker and mix well. Cook for 3½ hours.
3 Mix in the spinach and sprinkle over the cheese, then cook for a further 30 minutes, or until the cheese melts.

TOP TIP
When choosing spinach, go for baby leaves as the more mature leaves are more likely to be stringy.

A can of black beans can be the foundation of many hearty vegetarian meals, but this has to be my favourite.

CHIPOTLE BLACK BEAN STEW

SERVES 4
Vegetarian and *Freezer-friendly*

PREP TIME
10 minutes

COOK TIME
4 hours on low, plus 5 minutes

INGREDIENTS
1 tbsp olive oil
1 onion, finely chopped
2 garlic cloves, crushed
½ tbsp cumin seeds
½ tbsp smoked paprika
1 tbsp dried oregano
2 x 400g cans black beans,
   drained and rinsed
1 x 400g can chopped tomatoes
2 tbsp chipotle in adobo
60ml white wine vinegar
2 tbsp maple syrup (or brown sugar)
1 tbsp tomato purée
sea salt and black pepper

To serve

cooked rice
2 tomatoes, diced
a small handful of coriander,
   chopped
40g feta, crumbled

The smoky flavour from the paprika and chipotle and the creaminess from the beans make this a really comforting meal that freezes well and makes great leftovers too. Full of plant-based protein and fibre, this dish shows that vegetarian food can be both filling and cheap.

1 Preheat your slow cooker to low.
2 Heat the olive oil in a large frying pan over medium heat. Add the onion and garlic and gently cook for 3–4 minutes until softened.
3 Add the cumin, paprika and oregano to the pan and season with salt and pepper. Mix well and transfer to the slow cooker.
4 Add the rest of the ingredients and stir until well combined. Cook for 4 hours.
5 Serve on rice and top with the tomato, coriander and feta.

NUTRITION FACT
Black beans can help with pre-natal health. They contain high levels of folate, which is important for the healthy development of unborn babies.

If the bank balance and cupboards are looking a little bare towards the end of the month, then give this budget-busting sweet potato and egg curry a try.

SWEET POTATO AND EGG CURRY

SERVES 4
Vegetarian

PREP TIME
10 minutes

COOK TIME
5 hours on low, plus 5 minutes

INGREDIENTS
1 tbsp olive oil
1 large onion, diced
1 medium sweet potato, peeled and diced
2 garlic cloves, crushed
2 tbsp garam masala
½ tsp ground coriander
½ tsp ground cumin
½ crushed red chilli flakes
1 x 400g can chopped tomatoes
2 tbsp tomato purée
150ml vegetable stock
4 eggs
4 tbsp Greek yoghurt
a handful of fresh coriander, chopped
sea salt and black pepper

If you already have a well-stocked spice cupboard (an essential for healthy eating on a budget), then you just need a few extra ingredients for a cheap and filling meal that does not lack in nutrients. This was cooked at least twice a month when I was a student.

1 Preheat your slow cooker to low.
2 Heat the oil in a large frying pan over medium heat and add the onion and sweet potato. Gently cook for 2–3 minutes, then stir in the garlic, garam masala, ground coriander, cumin and red chilli flakes and cook for a further 1 minute.
3 Transfer everything to the slow cooker along with the chopped tomatoes, tomato purée and vegetable stock and season with salt and pepper. Cook for 5 hours until the sweet potato is cooked through.
4 Ten minutes before the end of the cooking time, add the eggs to a pan of boiling water and simmer for 10 minutes. Once cool enough to handle, peel the eggs and halve them.
5 Gently stir the eggs into the curry with the yoghurt and fresh coriander before serving.

If you are looking to add more vegan meals to your diet, then this is a really easy and flavourful one to start with. It has lots of texture to it and even meat eaters will be won over by this creamy and mild curry.

SWEET POTATO AND CHICKPEA CURRY

SERVES 2

Vegan, Freezer-friendly and
  Kid-approved

PREP TIME
10 minutes

COOK TIME
6 hours on low, plus 5 minutes

INGREDIENTS
1 tbsp olive oil
1 onion, diced
2 garlic cloves, crushed
1 tbsp finely diced fresh ginger
1 small sweet potato,
  peeled and diced
120g cooked chickpeas
200ml light coconut milk
juice of ½ a lime
2 tbsp curry powder
100ml vegetable stock
100ml passata
a handful of fresh coriander,
  chopped
sea salt and black pepper

1 Preheat your slow cooker to low.

2 Heat the oil a large frying pan over medium heat and cook the onion, garlic and ginger for 4 minutes, until softened.

3 Put the onion mixture in the slow cooker with the rest of the ingredients, season and cook for 6 hours until the sweet potato is cooked through.

4 Stir in the coriander before serving.

FUN FACT

Chickpeas are known by many different names all over the world. Other names include garbanzo beans, bengal grams, Egyptian peas, ceci beans and kabuli chana. Chickpeas can also be black, green, red and brown.

If you are a vegetarian, then chances are you have eaten this meal a few times in your life. But to me, it never gets boring and now it is even simpler cooked in a slow cooker.

MUSHROOM STROGANOFF

SERVES 2
Vegetarian and *Kid-approved*

PREP TIME
10 minutes

COOK TIME
3 hours on high

INGREDIENTS
500g mixed mushrooms, sliced
1 onion, thinly sliced
3 garlic cloves, crushed
200ml vegetable stock
1 tsp smoked paprika
4 tbsp 0% fat crème fraîche
a handful of fresh parsley,
    finely chopped, plus extra
    to serve
sea salt and black pepper
wild rice, to serve

A few substitutions make this creamy dish lower in fat and calories, but still packing in just as much flavour. Even meat eaters will enjoy it, due to the firm texture of the mushrooms. The key to adding plenty of texture to this dish is using a mix of mushrooms. This version used chestnut, shiitake and oyster mushrooms.

1 Preheat your slow cooker to high.
2 Add the mushrooms, onion, garlic, stock and paprika to the slow cooker and season with salt and pepper. Cook for 3 hours.
3 Remove a couple of spoonfuls of the liquid and add to the creme fraîche. Stir that mixture back into the slow cooker with the fresh parsley.
4 Serve the stroganoff with wild rice and a sprinkling of fresh parsley.

TOP TIP
Mushrooms should be wiped clean with a damp paper towel, then patted dry. Never soak mushrooms, as they absorb water and won't cook as well.

Get a taste of the Mediterranean with this hearty bean stew that can easily be adapted to make it vegan. We have made this a few times on a camping stove outside the tent after a long day of hiking, and it will warm you up whilst setting your taste buds alight.

MEDITERRANEAN BEAN AND BULGAR STEW

SERVES 2

Vegetarian, Freezer-friendly and *Kid-approved*

PREP TIME
5 minutes

COOK TIME
3 hours on high

INGREDIENTS
1 x 400g can cannellini beans, drained and rinsed
1 x 400g can chopped tomatoes
375ml vegetable stock
2 tbsp sundried tomato purée
15 pitted black olives, diced
80g bulgar wheat
2 garlic cloves, crushed
juice of ½ a lemon
1 tbsp dried oregano
1 tbsp dried marjoram
1 tbsp paprika
2 tbsp fresh parsley, finely chopped, plus extra to serve
a bag of mixed rocket and watercress leaves
sea salt and black pepper
40g feta, crumbled, to serve

If you wanted to give this dish even more of a protein boost, you could mix in some shredded chicken before serving.

1 Preheat your slow cooker to high.
2 Put the beans, tomatoes, stock, sundried tomato purée, black olives, bulgar wheat, garlic, lemon, oregano, marjoram, paprika and parsley in the slow cooker and season with salt and pepper.
3 Cook for 3 hours until the bulgur is cooked through.
4 Ten minutes before the end of the cooking time, stir in the rocket and watercress leaves.
5 Serve in bowls with the feta and extra parsley sprinkled on top.

The chunkiness and meaty texture of mushrooms make them a tasty vegetarian alternative to spaghetti bolognese.

MUSHROOM BOLOGNESE

SERVES 2

Vegan, Freezer-friendly and *Kid-approved*

PREP TIME
10 minutes

COOK TIME
8 hours on low, plus 5 minutes

INGREDIENTS
1 tbsp olive oil
1 onion, diced
1 large carrot, peeled and diced
1 celery stalk, diced
4 garlic cloves, crushed
12 closed cup mushrooms, finely chopped
2 tbsp dried oregano
4 tbsp balsamic vinegar
2 tbsp tomato purée
1 x 400g can chopped tomatoes
sea salt and black pepper
tagliatelle, to serve

Eating more meatless meals has countless health benefits and this family favourite has been given a vegetarian twist that the whole family will love. Keep it vegan, or sprinkle over some cheese to give it a creamy topping. With its rich and deeply flavourful sauce, you will not miss the beef from a traditional bolognese. Want to make this sauce even richer? Add a little glug of red wine before cooking.

1 Preheat your slow cooker to low.

2 Heat the oil a large frying pan over medium heat and cook the onion, carrot, celery and garlic for 3 minutes. Season with salt and pepper, stir, then transfer to the slow cooker.

3 Add the rest of the ingredients to the slow cooker and stir well. Put the lid on and cook for 8 hours until the mushrooms are cooked through.

4 Serve the sauce with tagliatelle.

This vegan lentil ragu is a delicious vegetarian alternative to spaghetti bolognese. It is bulked out with nutrient-rich lentils, so a bowl of this will leave you full and satisfied.

LENTIL RAGU

SERVES 4

Vegan, Freezer-friendly and *Kid-approved*

PREP TIME
10 minutes

COOK TIME
3 hours on high

INGREDIENTS
85g red lentils, rinsed
250ml vegetable stock
1 x 400g can chopped tomatoes
2 tbsp tomato purée
2 tbsp balsamic vinegar
3 garlic cloves, crushed
1 small onion, diced
2 tbsp dried oregano
1 large carrot, peeled and diced
1 celery stalk, diced
sea salt and black pepper
pasta of your choice, to serve
fresh parsley, chopped, to serve

This dish will also get you a little bit closer towards your five-a-day and, if you can believe it, it tastes even better as leftovers the next day. Either serve it on some freshly cooked pasta, or pile on top of a jacket potato.

1 Preheat your slow cooker to high.
2 Put everything in the slow cooker and stir well.
3 Cook for 3 hours until the lentils are cooked through.
4 Serve the ragu with pasta and a sprinkling of fresh parsley.

This dish is an easy way to add some extra greens to your diet and the kale goes nice and soft after being cooked for a long period of time.

WHITE BEAN AND KALE STEW

SERVES 4
Vegan and *Freezer-friendly*

PREP TIME
10 minutes

COOK TIME
3 hours on low

INGREDIENTS
1 x 400g can cannellini beans, drained and rinsed
250ml vegetable stock
1 x 400g can good-quality chopped tomatoes
2 tbsp tomato purée
1 carrot, peeled and chopped
1 celery stick, chopped
1 onion, diced
2 garlic cloves, crushed
1 tbsp dried thyme
1 tbsp dried oregano
½ tsp paprika
2 handfuls of chopped kale
sea salt and black pepper
French bread, to serve

Best served with a chunk of rustic French bread, you cannot get much better than this garlicky protein-packed vegetarian stew on a cold and grey day.

1 Preheat your slow cooker to low.
2 Put all of the ingredients, except the kale, in the slow cooker, season with salt and pepper and cook for 3 hours.
3 Twenty minutes before the end of the cooking time, stir in the kale.
4 Serve the stew in bowls with chunks of French bread.

Although chilli is traditionally meat-based, this vegan butternut squash and quinoa chilli can rival any meaty chilli in the taste department.

BUTTERNUT SQUASH AND QUINOA CHILLI

SERVES 4
Vegan and *Freezer-friendly*

PREP TIME
15 minutes

COOK TIME
6 hours on low, plus 5 minutes

INGREDIENTS
1 tbsp olive oil
1 onion, diced
1 celery stick, diced
1 green pepper, deseeded and diced
1 carrot, peeled and diced
2 garlic cloves, crushed
1 small butternut squash, peeled and diced
1 x 400g can cannellini beans, drained and rinsed
1 x 400g can chopped tomatoes
500ml vegetable stock
2 tbsp chipotle paste
1 tsp ground cumin
1 tsp paprika
1 tsp ground coriander
50g quinoa
juice of 1 lime
sea salt and black pepper
1 avocado, diced, to serve
a handful of fresh coriander, chopped, to serve

Chunks of butternut squash fill it out, the quinoa gives it plenty of protein, and you get a ton of smoky flavour from the chipotle that gives this vegan chilli the kick it needs. This dish is hearty enough to satisfy meat eaters and vegetarians/vegans alike.

1 Preheat your slow cooker to low.
2 Heat the oil in a frying pan over medium heat, then add the onion, celery, green pepper, carrot and garlic and gently cook for 4–5 minutes.
3 Add the onion mixture to the slow cooker with the butternut squash, beans, tomatoes, stock, chipotle paste, cumin, paprika, ground coriander, quinoa, lime juice and some seasoning. Cook for 6 hours until the butternut squash is cooked through.
4 Serve in bowls, topped with avocado and fresh coriander.

NUTRITIONAL FACT
Butternut squash is one of the most popular and versatile winter squashes, and that is not just down to its sweet and creamy taste. It is nutritionally dense, being a good source of vitamin A and the seeds being rich in protein and zinc. It also has a long storage life.

BONUS RECIPE
Use this chilli as a filling for tacos and top with guacamole for a vegan taco night that the whole family will love.

Possibly the easiest noodle dish you will ever make, and with the most vegetables packed into it, too.

VEGETABLE LO MEIN

SERVES 2
Vegetarian and *Kid-approved*

PREP TIME
15 minutes

COOK TIME
2¼ hours on high

INGREDIENTS
2 small carrots, peeled and
    cut into matchsticks
1 red pepper, deseeded and
    cut into matchsticks
1 celery stalk, chopped
10 baby corn, halved
½ head of broccoli, chopped
1 x 225g can water chestnuts,
    drained
200ml mushroom stock
1 tbsp sesame oil
2 tbsp light soy sauce
1 tbsp oyster sauce
1 tbsp honey
3 garlic cloves, crushed
a thumb-sized piece of ginger,
    peeled and grated
½ tsp red chilli flakes
125g dried egg noodles

This is another good recipe to clear out your fridge with, as you do not have to stick to the same vegetables each time – just add what needs using up. Slow cookers are amazing for helping you to reduce food waste. Smooth noodles and crunchy vegetables, this healthier alternative to a popular side dish will hit the spot if you are craving Chinese takeaway.

1 Preheat your slow cooker to high.
2 Put the carrots, red pepper, celery, baby corn, broccoli and water chestnuts in the slow cooker.
3 In a bowl, mix together the stock, sesame oil, soy sauce, oyster sauce, honey, garlic, ginger and chilli and stir well. Pour over the vegetables in the slow cooker and cook for 1½ hours until the vegetables are starting to soften.
4 Use a large spoon to gently push all the vegetables to one side, then add the noodles to the bottom of the slow cooker and spoon all the vegetables and sauce over them. Cook for a further 30 minutes, stir, then cook for another 15 minutes until the vegetables are cooked through but still have some bite.

TOP TIP
A good-quality soy sauce goes a long way in this dish. These noodles are really good cold the next day too.

This is a slow cooker twist on a French classic that goes a long way towards reducing food waste. We call this our fridge-raid ratatouille because it is what we always make the day before we go on holiday.

FRIDGE-RAID RATATOUILLE

SERVES 6

Vegan, Freezer-friendly and
   Kid-approved

PREP TIME
15 minutes

COOK TIME
6 hours on low

INGREDIENTS
1 onion, diced
2 peppers, deseeded and diced
1 aubergine, diced
2 courgettes, diced
1 head of broccoli, cut into chunks
2 celery sticks, diced
3 garlic cloves, crushed
8 chestnut mushrooms, sliced
2 tbsp dried oregano
1 tbsp dried basil
2 tbsp tomato purée
1 x 400g can chopped tomatoes
a handful of fresh basil,
   finely chopped
sea salt and black pepper

This recipe is really easy to adapt, which means you can use up all the vegetables that need eating before you go away and throw in any herbs you have to hand. This is a basic base recipe, so feel free to change it up.

1 Preheat your slow cooker to low.
2 Put all of the ingredients, except the fresh basil, in the slow cooker, season and mix well. Cook for 6 hours.
3 Stir in the fresh basil before serving.

FUN FACT
Ratatouille is a French Provençal stewed vegetable dish, originating in Nice, and is sometimes referred to as ratatouille niçoise.

Roasting vegetables really brings out the flavour, but so does cooking them in the slow cooker.

'ROASTED' VEGETABLE SALAD

SERVES 4
Vegetarian

PREP TIME
15 minutes

COOK TIME
3 hours on high

INGREDIENTS
2 small sweet potatoes,
  peeled and diced
1 red pepper, deseeded and diced
1 yellow pepper, deseeded
  and diced
1 red onion, cut into chunks
1 large courgette, cut into chunks
2 tbsp olive oil
1 tbsp garlic powder
1 tbsp dried oregano
1 tbsp dried basil
sea salt and black pepper

To serve

1 head of lettuce, chopped
8 pitted green olives, halved
8 pitted kalamata olives, halved
4 tbsp sunflower seeds
60g light feta, crumbled

Although you do not get the crispy edges that you do with roasting, this slow cooker version has just as much flavour, but without having to turn the oven on – perfect for a summer salad on a boiling hot day.

Just like the Fridge-raid Ratatouille (see page 173) this is a great dish to use up all your vegetables, because it is easily adaptable.

1 Preheat your slow cooker to high.
2 Put the sweet potato, red and yellow peppers, red onion, courgette, olive oil, garlic powder, oregano and basil in the slow cooker, season and mix well.
3 Cook for 3 hours until the vegetables are cooked but still have some bite. If you have a lot of liquid in the slow cooker after cooking, you can drain the vegetables.
4 Put the lettuce in bowls and top with the cooked vegetables, then sprinkle over the olives, sunflower seeds and feta before serving.

If you are feeling a bit tired of taco Tuesday, or burritos are becoming a bit boring, then why not change it up a bit and make some cheesy vegetable enchiladas.

SPINACH AND BLACK BEAN ENCHILADAS

SERVES 2

Vegetarian, Freezer-friendly and
Kid-approved

PREP TIME
10 minutes

COOK TIME
3 hours on low

INGREDIENTS
1 x 400g can black beans, drained
   and rinsed
100g fresh spinach, finely chopped
1 small onion, diced
2 garlic cloves, crushed
80g Cheddar, grated
½ tsp ground cumin
½ tsp paprika
½ tsp chilli powder
4 corn tortillas
½ recipe quantity Salsa
   (see page 203)
sea salt and black pepper

To serve

a handful of fresh coriander,
   chopped
4 tbsp guacamole
2 tbsp yoghurt
a large green salad

These are a great way to sneak in some extra vegetables, and with plenty of hearty black beans, meat eaters won't miss out. Unlike regular enchiladas, this slow cooker version requires no pre-cooking, so they could not be easier, or tastier. Substituting the standard sour cream for yoghurt also makes them a little lighter.

1 Preheat your slow cooker to low.
2 Put the black beans, spinach, onion, garlic, half the cheese, the cumin, paprika, chilli and some salt and pepper in a bowl and mix well.
3 Divide the mixture between the 4 tortillas, then carefully fold them up.
4 Put half the salsa in the slow cooker and gently place the folded up tortillas inside. Top with the rest of the salsa and the other half of the cheese.
5 Cook for 3 hours until the filling is cooked and the tortillas are starting to go a little crispy.
6 Sprinkle the enchiladas with coriander and serve with guacamole, yoghurt and salad.

Sides

Garlic Potato Wedges

Garlic and Lemon Asparagus

Greek Potatoes

Vegetable-Loaded Potatoes

Egg 'Fried' Rice

Moroccan Vegetable Couscous

Red Onion and Tomato Chutney

Sesame Brussels Sprouts

Honey and Mustard Sweet
Potato Mash

Whole Spiced Cauliflower

Garlic, Cauliflower and Potato Mash

Baba Ganoush

Salsa

Baked Beans

Mediterranean Rice

Spicy Almonds

If your oven is filled up with homemade burgers for burger night, then why not put the slow cooker to work to cover the side dishes?

GARLIC POTATO WEDGES

SERVES 4
Vegan and *Kid-approved*

PREP TIME
10 minutes

COOK TIME
6 hours on high

INGREDIENTS
4 medium white potatoes
4 tbsp olive oil
2 tbsp garlic powder
1 tbsp dried oregano
sea salt and black pepper
freshly snipped chives, to serve

'Crispy' and 'slow cooker' are not usually words that go together, but these garlic potato wedges get nice and crispy on the outside, while still remaining lovely and fluffy on the inside. If you want to take these wedges to the next level, then sprinkle some Parmesan cheese over them before cooking.

1 Preheat your slow cooker to high.
2 Cut the potatoes into wedges, put in a bowl with the rest of the ingredients apart from the chives and mix well.
3 Spray the inside of the slow cooker with oil and cook for 6 hours.
4 Sprinkle with fresh chives before serving.

NUTRITIONAL FACT
White potatoes have a bad reputation, but they can and should be part of a healthy balanced diet. They are a great source of vitamin B6, vitamin C, dietary fibre and potassium.

Garlic and lemon are the perfect flavour combination when it comes to asparagus. Just four ingredients go into making this really simple but flavour-packed side dish.

GARLIC AND LEMON ASPARAGUS

SERVES 4
Vegan

PREP TIME
5 minutes

COOK TIME
2 hours on high

INGREDIENTS
juice and zest of 1 lemon
3 garlic cloves, crushed
2 tbsp olive oil
20 asparagus spears
sea salt and black pepper

1 Preheat your slow cooker to high.
2 Put the lemon juice and zest, garlic and olive oil into a bowl, season and mix well.
3 Put the asparagus in the slow cooker and pour the liquid over it. Cook for 2 hours.

FUN FACT
When farmed, asparagus can't be harvested until three years after the seeds have been sown.

Realising you could perfectly cook potatoes in the slow cooker was probably one of my greatest slow cooking discoveries and we rarely cook them any other way now.

GREEK POTATOES

SERVES 4
Vegan and *Kid-approved*

PREP TIME
10 minutes

COOK TIME
4 hours on high

INGREDIENTS
cooking oil spray
32 baby potatoes, halved
2 tbsp olive oil
juice and zest of 1 lemon, plus extra zest to serve
3 garlic cloves, crushed
1 tbsp dried marjoram
1 tbsp dried oregano
10 fresh mint leaves, finely chopped, plus extra to serve
sea salt and black pepper

The flavour combinations are almost endless, but this Greek version with lemon zest and fragrant herbs is a favourite. The key to getting these nice and crisp is to use halved baby potatoes. With just a couple of minutes preparation you have yourself a winning side dish.

1 Preheat your slow cooker to high.

2 Line the slow cooker with foil leaving excess at the top, then spray with a little oil.

3 To a large bowl, add all the ingredients, seasoning to taste, and mix well. Pour into the slow cooker, then fold over the foil to allow the potatoes to steam.

4 Cook for 4 hours until the potatoes are cooked through, then serve with extra fresh mint and lemon zest.

Along with the nachos on page 131, these veggie-packed potatoes make great match-day food. Cheesy potatoes have been given a health kick by loading them with vegetables, hidden under the gooey cheese.

VEGETABLE-LOADED POTATOES

SERVES 4

Vegetarian and *Kid-approved*

PREP TIME
10 minutes

COOK TIME
4 hours on high

INGREDIENTS
cooking oil spray
24 baby potatoes (quartered)
1 yellow pepper, deseeded and diced
1 red pepper, deseeded and diced
1 small onion, diced
80g mature Cheddar, grated
2 tbsp garlic powder
2 tbsp oregano
sea salt and black pepper

To serve (optional)

Greek yoghurt
snipped chives
finely sliced spring onions

You can easily adapt this and make it different every time. A little bit of turkey bacon goes a long way on this, too. Put a big bowl of these on the table and watch everyone fight over them more than they fight over the result of the game.

1 Preheat your slow cooker to high.
2 Line the slow cooker with foil leaving excess at the top, then spray with a little oil.
3 Add half the potatoes, half the peppers and onion, half the garlic and half the oregano, and season with salt and pepper. Sprinkle over half the cheese.
4 Repeat to add another layer, finishing with the cheese, then fold the foil over the top of the potatoes. Cook for 4 hours until the potatoes are cooked through.
5 Serve with a few dollops of Greek yoghurt and a sprinkle of snipped chives and spring onions.

This is a lightened-up version of a classic takeaway side dish. It still has all the flavour that you love from egg fried rice, but it is slow cooked (using no oil) instead. It goes perfectly with the Sweet and Sour Chicken (page 69).

EGG 'FRIED' RICE

SERVES 4
Vegetarian

PREP TIME
10 minutes

COOK TIME
2 hours on high

INGREDIENTS
170g brown rice
375ml vegetable stock
2 tbsp soy sauce
2 garlic cloves, crushed
½ thumb-sized piece of ginger, peeled and grated
½ red onion, diced
1 carrot, diced
1 egg, beaten
a handful of frozen peas
a handful of frozen sweetcorn

1 Preheat your slow cooker to high.
2 Put all of the ingredients in the slow cooker and mix well.
3 Cook for 2 hours until the rice is cooked, stirring every 30 minutes.

Couscous is a pantry staple because it is so versatile, and not only does it make a great side dish, but it can be used to bulk out a main dish too.

MOROCCAN VEGETABLE COUSCOUS

SERVES 4
Vegetarian

PREP TIME
10 minutes

COOK TIME
4 hours on high, plus 5 minutes

INGREDIENTS
1 tbsp olive oil
1 onion, diced
2 garlic cloves, crushed
3 tbsp ras-el-hanout
1 courgette, diced
1 aubergine, diced
2 peppers (mixed colours),
   deseeded and diced
1 x 400g can chopped tomatoes
375ml vegetable stock
2 tbsp harissa
1 tbsp honey
juice and zest of ½ a lemon
150g couscous
1 x 210g can chickpeas, drained
   and rinsed
sea salt and black pepper

To serve

65g Greek yoghurt
2 tbsp tahini
a handful of fresh mint leaves,
   finely chopped
a handful of pomegranate seeds

Another great way to use Moroccan spice mixture ras-el-hanout, this vegetable-packed dish also makes a good addition to a BBQ or picnic, making a nice change from the standard potato or pasta salad.

1 Preheat your slow cooker to high.

2 Heat the oil in a frying pan over medium heat, then add the onion and garlic and gently cook for 2 minutes. Stir in the ras-el-hanout and cook for a further 1 minute.

3 Add the onion mixture to the slow cooker with the courgette, aubergine, peppers, tomatoes, stock, harissa, honey, lemon juice and zest and some seasoning, and cook for 4 hours.

4 Thirty minutes before it is ready, add the couscous and chickpeas and stir well.

5 Mix together the yoghurt and tahini and serve over the vegetable couscous with a sprinkle of fresh mint and pomegranate seeds.

If you have a jar of this in your fridge, the uses for it are almost endless. In an airtight jar, it will keep for around five days and it goes well on sandwiches and burgers and in salads, and is a must at any party you are throwing.

RED ONION AND TOMATO CHUTNEY

MAKES 12 PORTIONS
Vegan and *Kid-approved*

PREP TIME
10 minutes

COOK TIME
8 hours on low

INGREDIENTS
4 tomatoes, diced
2 red onions, thinly sliced
2 garlic cloves, crushed
2 tbsp maple syrup
50ml balsamic vinegar
100ml malt vinegar
50ml apple cider vinegar

1 Preheat your slow cooker to low.
2 Put all of the ingredients into the slow cooker. Cook for 8 hours, or until all the liquid has reduced and you have a thick chutney.

Brussels sprouts – you either love them or you hate them, and even haters have been swayed by these moreish little bites.

SESAME BRUSSELS SPROUTS

SERVES 2
Vegan

PREP TIME
5 minutes

COOK TIME
2 hours on high

INGREDIENTS
250g trimmed Brussels sprouts
2 tbsp sesame oil
2 tbsp balsamic vinegar
sea salt and black pepper

Either pile these sesame-flavoured sprouts high on your plate as a side dish, or just pick at them as a snack. This makes a nice alternative Christmas side dish, too, as even reluctant sprout eaters of the family will enjoy them.

1 Preheat your slow cooker to high.
2 Put all of the ingredients in the slow cooker and season with salt and pepper. Cook for 2 hours until the spouts have cooked through, but still have a little bite.

FUN FACT
Brussels sprouts have been grown in Belgium since the 13th century, which is where their name comes from, although the ancient Romans also grew them.

Mashed potato is always a go-to, easy side dish because it goes with almost everything. Creamy and comforting, this sweet mustard version makes a nice change from regular mash.

HONEY AND MUSTARD SWEET POTATO MASH

SERVES 4

Vegetarian and *Kid-approved*

PREP TIME
10 minutes

COOK TIME
4 hours on low

INGREDIENTS
3 medium sweet potatoes, peeled
   and chopped into chunks
a splash of skimmed milk
2 tbsp honey or maple syrup
3 tbsp wholegrain mustard
sea salt and black pepper
fresh parsley, chopped, to serve

1 Preheat your slow cooker to low.

2 Put the sweet potato chunks in the slow cooker. Add just enough boiling water to cover the sweet potatoes. Cook for 4 hours until the potatoes are tender.

3 Drain the potatoes and put them back in the slow cooker bowl. Mash until smooth (or still with some lumps if you prefer them that way). Stir in the rest of the ingredients and season with salt and pepper. Serve sprinkled with fresh chopped parsley.

There is so much more that you can do with cauliflower than cover it with cheese or have it with a roast dinner.

WHOLE SPICED CAULIFLOWER

SERVES 4
Vegan

PREP TIME
10 minutes

COOK TIME
3 hours on high

INGREDIENTS
2 tbsp olive oil
½ tsp ground cumin
½ tsp chilli powder
½ tsp coriander
½ tsp ground coriander
½ tsp paprika
sea salt and black pepper
1 large head of cauliflower

FOR THE YOGHURT DIP
a small tub (about 150g) of natural
    yoghurt (vegan if wished)
juice of ½ lemon
a small handful of mint leaves,
    chopped

You do not need to over-complicate things: simply add a mix of spices and some oil before slow cooking a cauliflower and you have yourself a delicious snack. That is right, a snack! Just break off chunks of this and dunk in a creamy yoghurt dip. Try putting this out for guests instead of crisps and sour cream next time you are having a gathering.

1 Preheat your slow cooker to high.
2 Combine the oil, spices and some salt and pepper in a small bowl.
3 Put the whole cauliflower in the slow cooker and rub the spice mixture over it. Cook for 3 hours until the cauliflower is tender when a knife is inserted into the thickest part.
4 To make the dip, mix together the yoghurt, lemon juice and fresh mint, and season with salt and pepper.
5 Serve the cauliflower with the dip and invite people to break off florets and dip them.

Potato mash is the ultimate comforting side dish,
but it can be a little heavy, especially if you are serving
it with a hearty main like a sausage casserole
(see page 66).

GARLIC, CAULIFLOWER AND POTATO MASH

SERVES 2

Vegetarian and *Kid-approved*

PREP TIME
10 minutes

COOK TIME
3 hours on high

INGREDIENTS
1 small head of cauliflower,
  chopped into florets
1 medium potato, peeled and
  chopped into chunks
2 garlic cloves, crushed
250ml vegetable stock
4 tbsp 0% fat Greek yoghurt
sea salt and black pepper

Keep the mash lighter by swapping out half the potato for
cauliflower, which is lower in carbs and adds some extra
flavour. Another sneaky vegetable dish, once the cauliflower is
mashed in with the potato and some garlic is added, you will
never be able to taste it. This is the ultimate hidden vegetable
side that still has all the creamy comfort of mashed potato.

1 Preheat your slow cooker to high.
2 Add all of the ingredients, except the yoghurt, to the slow
cooker and cook for 3 hours.
3 Use a hand blender to blend the mixture until smooth, then
stir in the yoghurt and season to taste before serving.

Hands down, baba ganoush is one of the best dips there is, and a great way to get more of your five-a-day.

BABA GANOUSH

SERVES 4
Vegan

PREP TIME
10 minutes

COOK TIME
2 hours on high

INGREDIENTS
1 aubergine, peeled and cut into
    small chunks
juice of 1 lemon
2 tbsp tahini
1 garlic clove, crushed
2 tbsp olive oil
sea salt and black pepper
flat-leaf parsley and pomegranate,
    to serve

This delicious smoky Middle Eastern aubergine dip is perfectly paired with some homemade pitta or flatbread and a sprinkle of pomegranate seeds. Like most great dishes, the ingredients list is simple and the flavour of the lemon juice and garlic really shine through. Although I'm not usually a huge fan of aubergines, this is one of my favourite things to eat.

1 Preheat your slow cooker to high.
2 Put the aubergine, lemon juice, tahini and garlic in the slow cooker with 4 tbsp of water and some seasoning.
Cook for 2 hours until the aubergine has softened.
3 Transfer the cooked aubergine to a food processor with the olive oil and blend until the desired consistency.
4 Serve with a sprinkling of parsley and pomegranate.

Jarred salsa might just be one of the most overpriced things on the market, when you look at how quick, easy and cheap it is to make yourself – especially if you have fresh summer tomatoes to use up.

SALSA

SERVES 8
Vegan

PREP TIME
10 minutes

COOK TIME
2 hours on high

INGREDIENTS
8 fresh tomatoes, quartered
4 garlic cloves, crushed
1 small red onion, diced
2 tbsp apple cider vinegar
juice of 1 lime
2 jalapeños, chopped (or the
    equivalent of jarred pickled
    jalapeños if you can not find
    fresh)
a large handful of fresh coriander,
    chopped
sea salt and black pepper
tortilla chips, to serve

Everyone makes salsa differently and whilst some think red onion is a must, others think salsa is nothing without some chopped-up pepper. This is my favourite simple salsa recipe that is zesty, spicy and has plenty of texture. A must at any party, with plenty of homemade tortilla chips to dunk in.

1 Preheat your slow cooker to high.
2 Put all of the ingredients except the coriander in the slow cooker and cook for 2 hours.
3 Just before it is done, add the coriander and stir well.
4 Leave to cool a little, then put the mixture in a blender and blend until the desired consistency. Season to taste.
5 Serve with tortilla chips.

BONUS RECIPE
Make your own tortilla chips by cutting flour tortillas into small triangles and putting on a baking tray. Spray with a little oil and sprinkle with a little sea salt, black pepper and garlic powder. Bake at 190ºC/Gas 5 for 3–4 minutes until crispy.

Ditch canned baked beans that are full of salt and sugar and make your own – it is really simple. Simply serve on some toast or in a jacket potato.

BAKED BEANS

SERVES 2

Vegan, Freezer-friendly and *Kid-approved*

PREP TIME
10 minutes

COOK TIME
4 hours on low, plus 5 minutes

INGREDIENTS
1 tbsp olive oil
½ small onion, diced
1 x 400g can cannellini beans, drained and rinsed
1 garlic clove, crushed
2 tsp maple syrup
50ml vegetable stock
250ml passata
2 tbsp tomato purée
1 tbsp apple cider vinegar
1 tsp mustard powder
½ tsp smoked paprika
sea salt and black pepper

1 Preheat your slow cooker to low.
2 Heat the oil in a frying pan over medium heat, add the onion and cook for 2 minutes.
3 Put the onion in the slow cooker with the rest of the ingredients and stir well.
4 Cook for 4 hours, stirring twice if possible. This is not a must though, as these can be set on a timer and cooked overnight. Season to taste before serving.

This is a variation of a side dish that we ate often during an island-hopping trip around Greece. It has been made many times since we got home, but in the slow cooker.

MEDITERRANEAN RICE

SERVES 6
Vegetarian

PREP TIME
15 minutes

COOK TIME
2 hours on high

INGREDIENTS
70g rice
250ml vegetable stock
2 garlic cloves, crushed
1 tbsp dried oregano
1 tbsp dried mint
1 tbsp dried marjoram
juice of 1 lemon
1 small onion, diced
sea salt and black pepper

To serve

1 yellow pepper, deseeded and diced
1 green pepper, deseeded and diced
12 cherry tomatoes, quartered
12 pitted kalamata olives,
   quartered
12 sundried tomatoes in oil, diced
60g light feta, crumbled
4 spring onions, sliced
a handful of fresh chives, snipped

Having never been able to perfect rice on the hob, I've found the slow cooker makes it perfectly fluffy. The saltiness of the olives and feta make a delicious topping for this herby and zesty rice dish.

1 Preheat your slow cooker to high.
2 Put the rice, stock, garlic, oregano, mint, marjoram, lemon juice and onion into the slow cooker. Season, mix well and cook for 2 hours.
3 Transfer to a serving bowl and add in all the remaining ingredients. Mix everything together well and serve.

Salty and crunchy snacks are sometimes all that get us through the day or keep us going until the next meal, but they do not have to be unhealthy. These spicy almonds are bursting with flavour and are a must with a cocktail at the weekend.

SPICY ALMONDS

SERVES 8
Vegan

PREP TIME
5 minutes

COOK TIME
2½ hours on low

INGREDIENTS
150g almonds (skins on)
1 tbsp melted coconut oil
sea salt and black pepper
1 tsp garlic powder
1 tsp paprika
1 tsp cayenne

They store and travel really well too, so we pack some when we go hiking for a protein-packed and calorie-dense snack. Do exercise portion control around these, though, because they are seriously addictive.

1 Preheat your slow cooker to low.
2 Put all the ingredients in the slow cooker and mix well.
3 Cook for 2½ hours, stirring every 30 minutes, until the almonds smell lovely and toasty.

FUN FACT
Almonds are part of the peach family. They are technically the hard-shelled fruit of the almond tree.

Desserts

Banana Bread

Chocolate Rice Pudding

Caramelised Bananas

Apple and Pear Crumble

A slice of this banana bread is the perfect afternoon pick-me-up. It uses oats rather than regular flour, so it would even make a nice Sunday breakfast treat. This recipe is a great way to use up bananas, too.

BANANA BREAD

SERVES 2

Vegetarian, Freezer-friendly and *Kid-approved*

PREP TIME
15 minutes

COOK TIME
2 hours on high

INGREDIENTS
200g rolled oats
½ tbsp bicarbonate of soda
1 tsp ground cinnamon
3 bananas
4 tbsp honey
4 tbsp melted coconut oil,
   plus extra for greasing
2 eggs
1 tsp vanilla extract
50g dark chocolate chips

1 Preheat your slow cooker to high.

2 Put the oats in a blender and blitz until they form a flour. Put the oat flour in a bowl with the bicarbonate of soda and cinnamon and mix.

3 In a separate bowl, mash the bananas. Add the honey, coconut oil, eggs and vanilla and whisk together.

4 Pour the wet mixture into the flour and mix well, then stir in the chocolate chips.

5 Grease your slow cooker with a little oil, then pour in the mixture. Cook for 2 hours, or until a skewer inserted into the middle of the bread comes out clean.

6 Leave to cool before running a knife around the edge of the slow cooker and turning the banana bread out.

It wasn't a good day when you were a kid unless it involved rice pudding. Forget about the cans of watery pudding and make some of this creamy rice pudding with a chocolate twist.

CHOCOLATE RICE PUDDING

SERVES 4
Vegetarian and *Kid-approved*

PREP TIME
5 minutes

COOK TIME
3 hours on high

INGREDIENTS
1 x 400ml can light coconut milk
500ml skimmed milk
170g pudding rice
3 tbsp maple syrup or honey
4 tbsp cocoa powder

1 Preheat your slow cooker to high.
2 Put all of the ingredients in the slow cooker and stir.
3 Cook for 3 hours until the rice is cooked.
4 Spoon into bowls to serve.

If banana bread is not your thing (see page 212), then this is another great way to use up bananas (although they cannot be too ripe for this recipe).

CARAMELISED BANANAS

SERVES 4
Vegan, Dairy-free and
  Kid-approved

PREP TIME
5 minutes

COOK TIME
2 hours on high

INGREDIENTS
1 tbsp melted coconut oil
3 tbsp maple syrup
½ tsp ground cinnamon
4 bananas
thick yoghurt, to serve (vegan,
  if wished)
desiccated coconut, to serve

These are sweet, soft and, with just a hint of coconut, go perfectly with some creamy thick yoghurt for a simple dessert.

1 Preheat your slow cooker to high.
2 Put the coconut oil, maple syrup and cinnamon into the slow cooker.
3 Slice each banana into 5 chunks, then add them to the slow cooker and gently mix well. Cook for 2 hours until the bananas have softened.
4 Serve the bananas with Greek yoghurt and a sprinkle of desiccated coconut.

FUN FACT
The old scientific name for banana is *musa sapientum*, which means 'fruit of the wise men'.

This dessert is a must on a cold Sunday afternoon after a roast dinner. It is super-comforting but without all the calories that usually come with comfort food. It is equally as tasty as a summer dessert with ice cream.

APPLE AND PEAR CRUMBLE

SERVES 4

Vegan, Freezer-friendly and
   Kid-approved

PREP TIME
10 minutes

COOK TIME
4 hours on low

INGREDIENTS
2 granny smith apples, peeled,
   cored and chopped into chunks
2 pears, peeled, cored and chopped
   into chunks
70g rolled oats
3 tbsp melted coconut oil
2 tbsp maple syrup
4 tbsp apple juice
½ tsp cinnamon
thick yoghurt, to serve (vegan,
   if wished)

1 Preheat your slow cooker to low.
2 Put the apples and pears in the slow cooker with the oats, coconut oil, maple syrup, apple juice and cinnamon and mix well. Cook for 4 hours until the apple and pear have softened.
3 Divide the crumble between bowls and serve with Greek yoghurt.

FUN FACT
Pears are part of the rose family and used to be called 'butter fruit' because of their soft butter-like texture.

Drinks

Coconut Hot Chocolate

Blackberry Juice Drink

Pumpkin Spiced Latte

Apple Chai Latte

This creamy coconut hot chocolate is thick and comforting and takes just five ingredients to make.

COCONUT HOT CHOCOLATE

SERVES 2
Vegetarian

PREP TIME
5 minutes

COOK TIME
2 hours on high

INGREDIENTS
500ml skimmed milk
250ml light coconut milk
3 tbsp honey
4 tbsp cocoa powder,
  plus optional extra to serve
35g dark chocolate
light squirty cream, to serve
  (optional)

Although it takes a little more effort than putting the kettle on and mixing hot water with powder, this hot drink is totally worth the extra couple of minutes it takes to put together. This is a family favourite for an indulgent way to start Christmas morning as we unwrap our presents.

1 Preheat your slow cooker to high.
2 Put all the ingredients in the slow cooker and whisk together. Cook for 2 hours, then stir again.
3 Pour into cups and top with squirty cream and a dusting of cocoa powder, if using, to serve.

BONUS RECIPE
Make different flavoured hot chocolates by adding either orange or peppermint extract.

Bottled fruit drinks can have a really long ingredients list, but this sweet fruity drink has just three and couldn't be easier. And what better way to use foraged blackberries in the autumn?

BLACKBERRY JUICE DRINK

SERVES 4
Vegan and *Kid-approved*

PREP TIME
5 minutes

COOK TIME
2½ hours on high

INGREDIENTS
200g blackberries
80ml maple syrup or honey

You can actually make this with any berries, and it is a great way to use up a glut of berries at the end of summer if you have been growing them yourself.

1 Preheat your slow cooker to high.
2 Put the blackberries in the slow cooker and mash to a pulp with a potato masher.
3 Stir in 500ml water and the maple syrup or honey and cook for 2½ hours.
4 Strain through a sieve, retaining the liquid and discarding the pulp.
5 Serve the drink undiluted.

All those visits to the coffee shop for a latte or cappuccino can soon add up, and even more so when everyone's favourite autumn drink makes its way back onto the menu.

PUMPKIN SPICED LATTE

SERVES 4
Vegan

PREP TIME
5 minutes

COOK TIME
2 hours on high

INGREDIENTS
500ml brewed coffee
500ml almond milk
6 tbsp pumpkin purée
4 tbsp maple syrup
¼ tsp ground cinnamon,
   plus extra to serve
¼ tsp ground ginger
¼ ground nutmeg
½ tsp vanilla extract
squirty cream to serve (optional)

Ready-made syrups have so many artificial ingredients in them, but you can easily make your own flavoured coffee with all natural ingredients. Save yourself some money and calories by making your own hot drink that is perfect for snuggling up with on a cold afternoon – and you do not even need to leave the house for it. Leave out the squirty cream for a vegan option.

1 Preheat your slow cooker to high.
2 Put all of the ingredients into the slow cooker, stir and cook for 2 hours.
3 Pour into glasses and serve topped with squirty cream, if using, and a sprinkle of cinnamon.

Originating in India, chai is a warming spiced drink that has gained popularity all over the world, and features on the menu in every popular coffee shop.

APPLE CHAI LATTE

SERVES 4
Vegetarian

PREP TIME
5 minutes

COOK TIME
4 hours on high

INGREDIENTS
2 tbsp honey
1 large apple, diced
4 black tea bags
a thumb-sized piece of ginger, peeled and sliced
5 cardamom pods, split open
4 black peppercorns
2 cinnamon sticks
2 star anise
7 whole cloves
500ml skimmed milk, warmed
cinnamon, to garnish

Whilst you can buy chai tea bags, if you have a good selection of spices in your cupboard you can make your own chai lattes at a fraction of the price. This autumn-inspired chai latte is a favourite in our house on bonfire night, or we put it on before going for a long autumnal walk, knowing we are coming home to a nice warming drink.

1 Preheat your slow cooker to high.
2 Put all of the ingredients, except the milk, into the slow cooker. Add 1 litre of water, stir and cook for 4 hours.
3 Strain the mixture, reserving the liquid and discarding the spices.
4 Divide the chai latte between mugs and top with the warmed milk. Serve sprinkled with cinnamon.

Index